Steck-Vaughn

Think-Alongs™
Comprehending As You Read

Level A

Teacher's Edition

Program Authors

Senior Author
Roger Farr

Co-Authors
Jennifer Conner
Elizabeth Haydel
Bruce Tone
Beth Greene
Tanja Bisesi
Cheryl Gilliland

STECK-VAUGHN
C O M P A N Y

A Division of Harcourt Brace & Company

www.steck-vaughn.com

Acknowledgments

Editorial Director	Diane Schnell
Project Editor	Anne Souby
Associate Director of Design	Cynthia Ellis
Design Manager	Ted Krause
Production and Design	Julia Miracle-Hagaman
Photo Editor	Claudette Landry
Product Manager	Patricia Colacino
Cover Design	Ted Krause
Cover Sculpture	Lonnie Springer
Cover Production	Alan Klemp

Think-Alongs™ is a trademark of Steck-Vaughn Company.

ISBN 0-7398-0089-2

Contents

Program Overview

We have all had the experience of reading a page and then not remembering what we read. For those of us who are good readers, this experience only occurs once in a while, when we are distracted and thinking about something else. But for newer readers or poor readers, this experience occurs repeatedly. They read the words on the page without making connections or visualizing what they are reading. They *are* reading, but they are not comprehending. For these students, and for all of us at times, it can be too easy to read the words on the page without thinking about the meaning of those words.

How can you encourage students to think while they read?

The **Steck-Vaughn Think-Alongs™: Comprehending As You Read** series is designed to provide you with a tool to do just that. In this series, students will learn to engage in a process called "thinking along." Whether students are thinking aloud or responding to written questions, the activities in this series will help them think as they read. By practicing the strategies presented here,

students will become better comprehenders of the variety of texts they will encounter in school, in testing situations, and in their personal lives. These reading comprehension and critical thinking strategies will help students understand all texts, both expository and narrative, and help them feel successful about reading.

The **Steck-Vaughn Think-Alongs: Comprehending As You Read** series is designed to provide opportunities for students to:

- Think and comprehend as they read.
- Learn the reading strategies needed to become more effective comprehenders.
- Practice effective reading strategies with a variety of texts.

- Construct meaning as they read.
- Become more effective in their use of metacognitive reading strategies.
- Connect what they know to what is being read.
- Develop techniques that promote more effective reading.
- Write while reading, thus encouraging them to think about the text.
- Discuss the story and internalize unfamiliar vocabulary.
- Learn to use ideas developed while reading to write more effectively.
- Practice thinking strategies that can be used to improve reading comprehension test-taking skills.

The activities in this book are designed to work with your classroom goals and schedule. The activities are flexible and can be adjusted to suit your students' needs and your personal teaching style. The program provides a way for you to model the think-along process for students by using the "Introducing Thinking Along" section on pages T12–T15. The student books are easy to use, and the teacher's edition provides numerous activities for introducing, discussing, and extending each of the selections.

About the Author

Dr. Roger Farr, program author of Steck-Vaughn Think-Alongs: Comprehending As You Read, has been working on the strategies in this program for more than a decade. He has conducted hundreds of workshops and seminars with teachers over the years, has been directly involved with students in applying these strategies, and has received feedback from many teachers who have used the techniques in their classrooms. Dr. Farr has applied this research to **Think-Alongs**, thus developing effective and easy-to-use strategies for both teaching and learning reading comprehension.

A teacher of kindergarten through graduate school, Dr. Farr is a senior author of *Signatures* and *Collections*, both K-6 reading programs from Harcourt School Publishers, and he also serves as a special consultant to Harcourt on assessment and measurement. He is Chancellors' Professor of Education and Director of the Center for Innovation in Assessment at Indiana University.

Dr. Farr is a former president of the International Reading Association. In 1984, the IRA honored Dr. Farr for outstanding lifetime contributions to the teaching of reading. In the same year, he was elected to the IRA Reading Hall of Fame, and in 1988 he was selected by the IRA as the Outstanding Reading Teacher Educator.

Components

The series consists of six pupil's editions for grades one through six and six accompanying annotated teacher's editions, as well as a video simulating actual classroom use. The Level A teacher's edition includes three Steck-Vaughn *Pair-It Books*® to facilitate an introduction to the think-along process.

Pupil's Editions

The pupil's editions are divided into four units in Levels A–C and three units in Levels D–F. Each unit of three selections introduces and then provides practice for a specific reading comprehension strategy. In Level A, students follow a logical progression from drawing to writing responses to think-along questions. As they work through the units, their comprehension skills increase. In the first and second units, you read the stories aloud, pausing at intervals to ask students think-along questions. In the third and fourth units, students read to themselves, pausing at intervals to draw or write responses to questions in "think-break" boxes. The questions are different from many traditional reading questions in that there are no correct or incorrect responses. Students are encouraged to think about the text in their own way.

In addition, the pupil's editions include two sections that allow students to apply the think-along process to test-taking situations. These sections consist of three reading passages, followed by multiple-choice and open-ended questions modeled after standardized tests. A sample question is provided so you may practice test-taking strategies with students. In addition, a purpose-setting question leads students to focus. These practice sections help improve students' test-taking skills.

Pupil's Edition Features

Strategies for thinking along are introduced and modeled. Students are given ample practice thinking along with real literature and then responding in writing.

The pupil's edition includes:

- *Introduction to the Strategy*
- *Reading Selection*
- *Writing Activity*
- *Test-Taking Practice*

Introduction to the Strategy

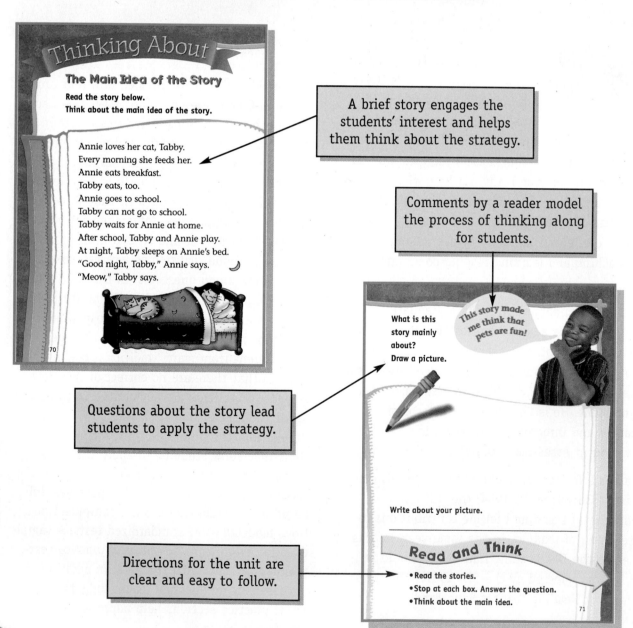

Thinking About

The Main Idea of the Story

Read the story below.
Think about the main idea of the story.

Annie loves her cat, Tabby.
Every morning she feeds her.
Annie eats breakfast.
Tabby eats, too.
Annie goes to school.
Tabby can not go to school.
Tabby waits for Annie at home.
After school, Tabby and Annie play.
At night, Tabby sleeps on Annie's bed.
"Good night, Tabby," Annie says.
"Meow," Tabby says.

70

A brief story engages the students' interest and helps them think about the strategy.

Comments by a reader model the process of thinking along for students.

What is this story mainly about?
Draw a picture.

This story made me think that pets are fun!

Questions about the story lead students to apply the strategy.

Write about your picture.

Read and Think

Directions for the unit are clear and easy to follow.

- Read the stories.
- Stop at each box. Answer the question.
- Think about the main idea.

71

Reading Selection

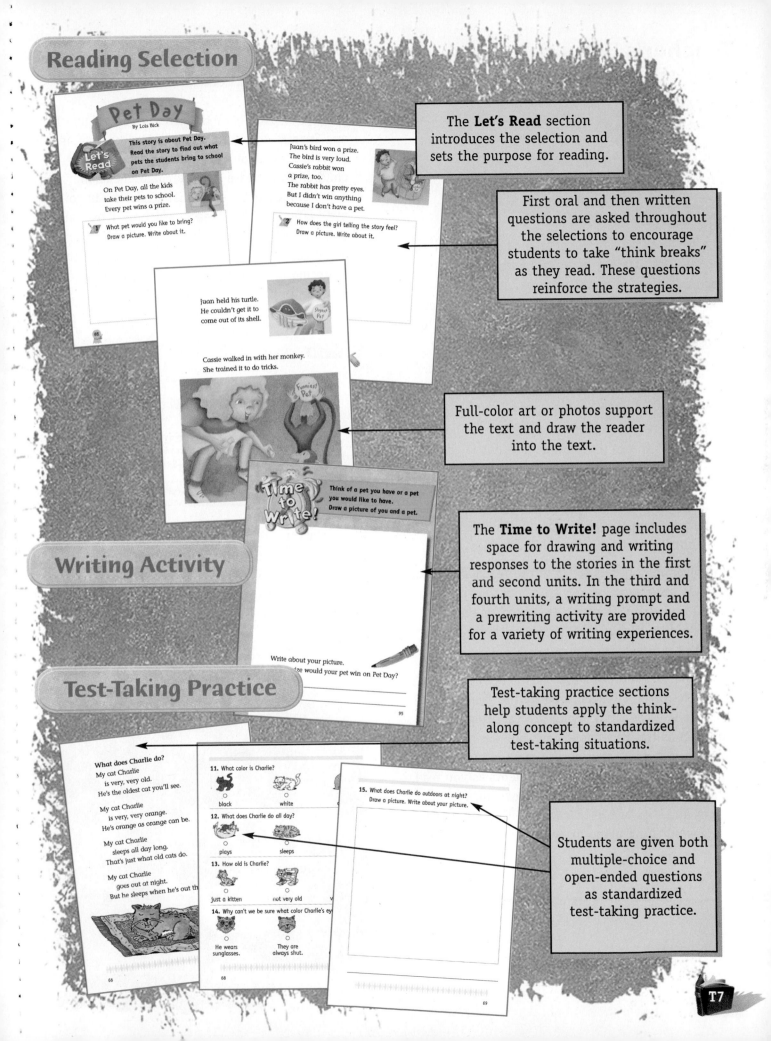

Pet Day
By Lois Bick

Let's Read

This story is about Pet Day. Read the story to find out what pets the students bring to school on Pet Day.

On Pet Day, all the kids take their pets to school. Every pet wins a prize.

1 What pet would you like to bring? Draw a picture. Write about it.

Juan's bird won a prize. The bird is very loud. Cassie's rabbit won a prize, too. The rabbit has pretty eyes. But I didn't win anything because I don't have a pet.

2 How does the girl telling the story feel? Draw a picture. Write about it.

Juan held his turtle. He couldn't get it to come out of its shell.

Cassie walked in with her monkey. She trained it to do tricks.

88

The **Let's Read** section introduces the selection and sets the purpose for reading.

First oral and then written questions are asked throughout the selections to encourage students to take "think breaks" as they read. These questions reinforce the strategies.

Full-color art or photos support the text and draw the reader into the text.

Time to Write!

Think of a pet you have or a pet you would like to have. Draw a picture of you and a pet.

Write about your picture.
...ze would your pet win on Pet Day?

95

Writing Activity

The **Time to Write!** page includes space for drawing and writing responses to the stories in the first and second units. In the third and fourth units, a writing prompt and a prewriting activity are provided for a variety of writing experiences.

Test-Taking Practice

Test-taking practice sections help students apply the think-along concept to standardized test-taking situations.

What does Charlie do?

My cat Charlie
is very, very old.
He's the oldest cat you'll see.

My cat Charlie
is very, very orange.
He's orange as orange can be.

My cat Charlie
sleeps all day long.
That's just what old cats do.

My cat Charlie
goes out at night.
But he sleeps when he's out th...

66

11. What color is Charlie?

○ black   ○ white

12. What does Charlie do all day?

○ plays   ○ sleeps

13. How old is Charlie?

○ just a kitten   ○ not very old

14. Why can't we be sure what color Charlie's ey...

○ He wears sunglasses.   ○ They are always shut.

68

15. What does Charlie do outdoors at night? Draw a picture. Write about your picture.

69

Students are given both multiple-choice and open-ended questions as standardized test-taking practice.

Teacher's Edition

The teacher's edition provides suggestions for introducing each strategy as well as a lesson plan for each selection. The teacher's edition also includes reduced pupil pages with possible student responses and suggestions for how to interpret and react to those responses. These suggestions indicate the strategies that the student responses reflect.

Highlighted throughout the teacher's edition are three types of additional activities:

- **ESOL** activities include suggestions for helping students whose first language is not English apply the think-along strategies.
- **Meeting Individual Needs** activities address the needs of students with different learning styles.
- **Reinforcing the Strategies** helps students maintain previously learned strategies.

In addition, pages T12–T15 of the teacher's edition include directions for how to model the think-along process by thinking aloud so students can think along. Part of this demonstration includes coached practice for students.

Three Steck-Vaughn *Pair-It Books*® are provided with the Level A teacher's edition to facilitate introducing the think-along process. Because the art is essential to students' comprehension and increases their interest in the reading process, it is important to show it to your students as you read aloud. Reduced pages of these books appear on pages T17–T28 of the teacher's edition, along with suggested think-along questions.

Blackline Masters

The teacher's edition contains several blackline masters:

- A letter to parents or caregivers in both English and Spanish to inform them of the program and provide suggestions for interacting with their children to increase reading comprehension.
- A self-assessment master that students can complete after they finish each selection. This evaluative tool helps students focus on metacognition and their attitudes about the think-along process.
- A scoring rubric for you to track students' progress in thinking along.

Video

A video accompanying the program features an introduction to the think-along process by Roger Farr and shows the program in use in actual classroom settings at several grade levels. It serves as a staff development tool for inservice or training purposes.

Teacher's Edition Features

The teacher's edition provides a wealth of information to enhance students' interaction with text through reading, writing, and discussion. At a glance, teachers can see a reduced pupil page. The program allows minimal preparation time and offers suggestions for maximizing instruction.

The teacher's edition features:

- *Before Reading Activities*
- *Possible Responses*
- *Helpful Tips*
- *After Reading Activities*

Before reading activities include:

- a clearly stated strategy,
- a summary of the selection for quick reference,
- a vocabulary list of unfamiliar words or words critical to understanding,
- suggestions for introducing the selection, and
- the purpose for reading.

Possible student responses demonstrate what to watch for and how to determine which strategies are being used. Questions are provided to further enhance student learning.

Helpful suggestions for meeting the individual needs of students, including those whose first language is not English, are given throughout the selections.

After reading activities include:

- suggestions for additional activities related to the selection strategy in the first and second units, and suggestions for leading a discussion of students' written responses in the third and fourth units.
- suggestions for reteaching the strategy to give additional options for student learning in the third and fourth units.

Each selection includes a list of additional activities and books on the topic to provide resources for further student interaction.

The writing section identifies ways for students to share what they have written.

Research Supporting Think-Along Strategies

Research during the past several decades has demonstrated that when students interact with text while reading, reading comprehension has improved. The impact of response techniques has been demonstrated in research involving reciprocal teaching, comprehension monitoring, think-aloud strategies, and writing in response to reading.

Do oral and written think-along activities help students understand what they are reading?

Ample research evidence demonstrates that active reasoning while reading enhances reading comprehension. Research has demonstrated the positive effects on reading comprehension when teachers ask thought-provoking questions while students are learning to read and when reading increasingly difficult new texts. Finally, numerous studies have demonstrated that good readers are active thinkers while reading.

Davey, Beth. **Think aloud—modeling the cognitive process of reading comprehension.** *Journal of Reading*, 27 (1), October 1983, pp. 44-47.

Kucan, Linda and Isabel L. Beck. **Four fourth graders thinking aloud: an investigation of genre effects**, *Journal of Literacy Research*, 28 (2), June 1996, pp. 259-287.

Loxterman, Jane. A, Isabel L. Beck, and Margaret G. McKeown. **The effects of thinking aloud during reading on students' comprehension of more or less coherent text.** *Reading Research Quarterly*, 29 (4), October-December 1994, pp. 352-367.

Pressley, Michael and Peter Afflerbach. ***Verbal Protocols of Reading: The Nature of Constructively Responsive Reading.*** Hillsdale, NJ: Lawrence Erlbaum Associates, 1995.

Does verbal or written interaction before and after reading enhance a reader's comprehension?

The research literature has documented the importance of a reader's active interaction with text—not only during reading, but also before and after reading. Readers who read with a purpose and discuss, write, and draw in active response to text are significantly better comprehenders than those who are passive readers.

McMahon, Susan I. and Taffy E. Raphael. ***The Book Club Connection.*** New York: Teachers' College Press, 1997.

Ogle, Donna. **Developing problem solving through language arts instruction.** In Collins, Cathy and John N. Mangieri (Eds.) *Teaching Thinking: An Agenda for the Twenty-First Century*. Hillsdale, NJ: Lawrence Erlbaum Associates, 1992, pp. 25-39.

Palincsar, Annemarie Sullivan and Ann L. Brown. **Reciprocal teaching of comprehension—fostering and comprehension monitoring activities.** *Cognition and Instruction*, 1 (2), 1984, pp. 117-125.

Does being aware of reading strategies help a reader comprehend more effectively and easily?

Awareness of reading strategies and how one is comprehending is called metacognition. The research on the positive impact of metacognitive strategies on reading comprehension is well documented.

Baker, Linda and Ann L. Brown. **Metacognitive skills and reading.** In Pearson, David P. (Ed.) *Handbook of Reading Research*. New York: Longman, 1984, pp. 353-394.

Farr, Roger, et al. **Writing in response to reading.** *Educational Leadership*, 47 (6), March 1990, pp. 66-69.

Paris, Scott G., Barbara A. Wasik, and Gert Van der Westhuizen. **Meta-metacognition: a review of research on metacognition and reading.** In Readence, John E. et al. (Eds.) *Dialogues in Literacy Research: Thirty-seventh Yearbook of The National Reading Conference*, National Reading Conference, 1988, pp. 143-166.

Raphael, Taffy E. and Clydie A. Wonnacott. **Heightening fourth-grade students' sensitivity to sources of information for answering comprehension questions.** *Reading Research Quarterly*, 20 (3), Spring 1985, pp. 282-296.

Tips for Using Think-Alongs in Your Classroom

An important aspect of using **Think-Alongs** in your classroom is to monitor and discuss students' responses to the think-along questions. The following tips will help you encourage and direct students in using **Think-Alongs.**

- Give positive feedback to student responses.

- Ensure that all students are responding to questions asked verbally or in the think-along boxes in the text. If they cannot answer a question, have them say, draw, or write whatever they are thinking.

- Assure students that there are no wrong answers. Answers will vary because students are making their own connections with the text.

- If students are unable to write an answer to a question in the fourth unit, encourage them to draw a picture. This is a particularly good strategy to use with students whose primary language is not English.

- The amount students write in the third and fourth units is not important. They do not have to write complete sentences.

- Encourage students to write or draw their ideas in the boxes fairly quickly and then continue reading the selection.

- Spelling, grammar, and punctuation are not as important as thinking and responding.

- Students may use a variety of strategies as they respond to questions.

- If students write or draw answers that are not clearly related to the selection, follow up by asking them why they wrote or drew what they did.

- If students do not understand the meaning of a word, encourage them to figure it out from the story's context or from hints in the illustrations.

- Model the think-along process at a specific place in a selection to help any student struggling with the process.

Scoring the Tests

First-grade students may be unfamiliar with the format of multiple-choice tests, and you should not be overly concerned with the scores on this test. However, you can use the students' performance on these tests to get an idea of how well students are comprehending, and to assist you in planning further instruction.

For each test, score 1 point for each multiple-choice question correct (total 12) and 2 points for each open-ended response (total 6). Add the two for a total of up to 18 points for the test. Refer to the information below for how to interpret the raw score.

Interpreting Test Scores

Raw Score	Planning Further Instruction
16-18	Excellent. These students are comprehending and should be encouraged to read independently and be exposed to thinking-along with new genres and content-area materials.
13-15	Good. These students are comprehending but may need some assistance going beyond a literal understanding of the story. Encourage these students to write, draw, and/or discuss what they are thinking while reading.
10-12	Satisfactory. These students need to be read aloud to and need additional practice thinking-along while reading.
Below 10	Needs improvement. These students will benefit from being read aloud to and using oral think-alongs in small groups.

Introducing Thinking Along

The following warm-up activities are optional. Feel free to modify the activities to meet your teaching goals and students' needs. These activities introduce your students to what it means to think along while reading. These activities will be valuable for all of your students, but especially for those who have difficulties comprehending what they read.

Activity 1
Modeling

Think aloud so your students can think along!

First, model thinking along with your students by thinking aloud while you read the book *A Fishy Story*. You will also find reduced pages from the book on pages T17–T20 of the teacher's edition.

The reduced pages are accompanied by suggested think-along questions, or you may offer questions of your own as you read the story aloud.

Read the Story Aloud

"I dreamed I caught a fish as big as a man."

In her next dream, I think she will catch a fish as big as a bear!

TIPS

If you want to use a different story or substitute your own statements to model thinking along, keep these tips in mind:

- Think aloud every sentence or two.
- Use a variety of strategies when you think aloud.
- Think aloud only at the end of a sentence, not in the middle of a sentence.

Activity 2
Providing Coached Practice

Get students to think along by asking specific questions.

Next, have students start thinking along with a story. Read *Going to the Pool* aloud to students. You will also find reduced pages from the book on pages T21–T24 of the teacher's edition. The reduced pages are accompanied by suggested think-along questions, or you may offer questions of your own as you read the story aloud.

Read the Story Aloud

"Rick's mom is going to the pool."

How do you think the pool looks?

I think the pool looks crowded.

TIPS

The teacher's edition provides questions that encourage students to use the following strategies with *Going to the Pool*:

- Prediction
- Personal Experience
- Visualization

Activity 3
Providing More Coached Practice

Get students to think along by asking, "What are you thinking about now?"

Next, have students think along by asking them the more general question, "What are you thinking about now?" Read *Whistle Like a Bird* aloud to students. You will also find reduced pages of the book on pages T25–T28.

After reading, have students draw a picture of their favorite part of the story. Ask them to tell about their pictures and explain why the scene they drew was their favorite part.

Read the Story Aloud

"Grandma shows me how to whistle like a bird."

What are you thinking about now?

I'm thinking that I'm a really good whistler.

TIPS

- If a student has trouble answering the general "What are you thinking about now" question, ask a more specific question, such as "What might happen next?"
- Have several students tell you what they are thinking about each time you stop.
- After a few students have shared their thoughts, share your own as well.

T14

Reflecting

• •

Get students to reflect on their responses and on the process of thinking along.

Next, have students think about their responses to the questions and how they feel about the process of thinking along. Respond to students' answers in a positive way, but if their answers seem unrelated to the reading, ask for clarification. Point out the strategies they are using. Note the individual approaches they are taking to show that many different answers are acceptable.

Finally, ask students how they feel about using the think-along process.

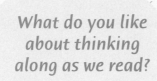

What do you like about thinking along as we read?

Thinking along is fun. It makes me think of things I don't usually think about when we read stories.

TIPS

To get students to support their responses:

- "That's an interesting idea. What made you think of that?"
- "I think I know what you mean. Can you explain a little more?"
- "I never thought of that. What made you think of that?"
- "I like that idea. Where did it come from?"

To get students to diversify their responses:

- "What an interesting idea! No one else thought of that."
- "Who else has another way of thinking about the story?"

To get students to use different strategies:

- "What do you think will happen next?"
- "What does the story remind you of?"
- "What picture does this make in your mind?"

Additional Think-Along Activities and Resources

Engaging Young Readers in Thinking Along

In order to familiarize younger students with the idea of thinking along while reading, you might start by using pictures before using texts to prompt think-along responses. Practicing with pictures will help your students feel comfortable with the idea of sharing what they are thinking about and with thinking beyond what they see, hear, or read.

Show your students some interesting pictures without captions and ask them to tell you what they are thinking about. Use pictures that encourage a variety of interpretations and thoughts. Using pictures will reinforce the idea that there are no right or wrong answers when you are thinking about a story.

A picture such as the following would work well to motivate students in the think-along process:

From *The Runaway Wheels*. Written by Stephanie Handwerker. Illustrated by Terry Kovalcik. Steck-Vaughn, 1997.

Ask students to tell you what they are thinking about when they look at the picture. To elicit a wide range of responses, ask students questions such as the following:

- *How do you think the boy in the picture feels? Why?*
- *What do you think is going to happen next?*
- *What do you think just happened?*

Remind students that thinking about pictures and stories in different ways will make them more interesting and easy to understand.

Recommended Books to Use with Think-Along Strategies

Your students will want to continue using the reading strategies presented in Level A with other books that they read. The think-along strategies can be used with any book. The following books work particularly well with the strategies introduced in this book.

Retell by Drawing Pictures

Good Dog Carl by Alexandra Day (Aladdin, 1997). In this mostly wordless story, a dog named Carl watches the baby while the mother is away.

I Went Walking by Sue Williams (Red Wagon, 1996). A child goes for a walk and is soon followed by a parade of brightly colored animals.

Peter Spier's Rain by Peter Spier (Yearling, 1997). This wordless picture book captures the wonder of a brother and sister's day together in the rain.

Connect Personal Experiences

My Best Friend by Pat Hutchins (Greenwillow, 1993). A girl's best friend can do many things better than she can—but still needs her friendship.

The Snowy Day by Ezra Jack Keats (Viking Press, 1981). A small boy enjoys playing in the freshly fallen snow.

Tomorrow Is Daddy's Birthday by Ginger Wadsworth (Boyds Mills Press, 1994). A girl tells everyone but Daddy about his surprise birthday gift.

Identify the Main Idea

Clifford, the Big Red Dog by Norman Bridwell (Scholastic, 1988). The first book in the Clifford series introduces Emily Elizabeth and her big red dog Clifford.

The Dog Who Cried Woof by Nancy Coffelt (Harcourt Brace, 1995). Children will recognize this retelling of the original "Cry Wolf" tale in the story of Ernie the dog, who annoys people with his loud, nonstop barking.

No Good in Art by Miriam Cohen (Yearling Books, 1996). A first grade boy thinks that he cannot draw—then realizes that with practice he can.

Make Predictions

The Carrot Seed by Ruth Krauss (HarperCollins Children's Books, 1988). A patient child waits for a seed to grow, watching it become a giant carrot.

Frog and Toad Together by Arnold Lobel (HarperTrophy, 1979). Frog and Toad do all kinds of things together, including planting a garden and sharing cookies.

Hi by Ann Herbert Scott (Philomel Books, 1994). A girl says "hi" to all the people at the post office until one person responds.

A Fishy Story

By Richard Leslie

On Monday I dreamed I caught a fish.
It was as big as a bird.

2

On Tuesday I dreamed I caught a fish.
It was as big as a cat.

3

Suggested Think-Along Teacher Response:

I'm thinking my brother once caught a fish that was about as big as a bird.

On Wednesday I dreamed I caught a fish.
It was as big as a dog.

4

On Thursday I dreamed I caught a fish.
It was as big as a man.

5

Suggested Think-Along Teacher Response:

In her next dream, I think she will catch a fish as big as a bear!

On Friday I dreamed I caught a fish.
It was as big as a horse.

6

On Saturday I dreamed I caught a fish.
It was as big as a whale.

7

Suggested Think-Along Teacher Response:

I'm thinking that I have never seen a fish that big. It must have been really heavy!

On Sunday I really went fishing.
I caught a little, tiny fish.

8

Suggested Think-Along Teacher Response:

Even though she dreamed she would catch a bigger fish, I think the girl is still happy with the little fish she caught.

Going to the Pool

By Ena Keo

Meg gets ready to go to the pool.

2

Meg's dad is going to the pool, too.

3

Suggested Think-Along Teacher Response:

What are some things you think Meg and her dad will bring with them to the pool?

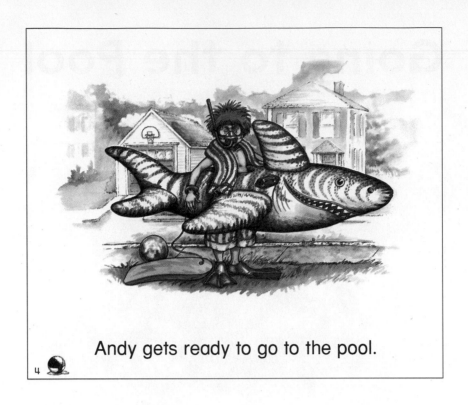

Andy gets ready to go to the pool.

4

Andy's mom is going to the pool, too.

5

Suggested Think-Along Teacher Response:

If you could go to a pool, who would go with you?

Rick gets ready to go to the pool.

6

Rick's mom is going to the pool, too.

7

Suggested Think-Along Teacher Response:

How do you think the pool looks?

But no one gets into the pool.

8

Suggested Think-Along Teacher Response:

How do you think they feel now that they can't get into the pool?

Whistle Like a Bird

By Sarah Vazquez

I want to whistle like a bird.

2

Grandma shows me how to whistle like a bird.

3

Suggested Think-Along Teacher Response:

What are you thinking about now?

I want to howl like a dog.

4

Grandma shows me how to howl like a dog.

5

Suggested Think-Along Teacher Response:

What are you thinking about now?

I want to sing like a star.

6

Grandma shows me how to sing like a star.

7

Suggested Think-Along Teacher Response:

What are you thinking about now?

Together we make a concert.

8

Suggested Think-Along Teacher Response:

What are you thinking about now?

At Home

Dear family of _____ ,

Our class has begun to read stories in a book titled **Steck-Vaughn Think-Alongs™: Comprehending As You Read.** The book uses an approach to reading called "thinking along." Your child will be answering questions and will be drawing and writing responses as the class reads a variety of stories. This process will help your child better understand and remember what he or she reads.

You can help your child in many ways. Ask your child about the stories and what he or she thinks about the drawing and writing exercises. Ask how your child feels about thinking along while reading. It is especially important to read with your child, stopping as you read to discuss a story. Ask questions such as, "What has just happened?" and "What do you think might happen next?" to strengthen your child's thinking skills.

Encourage your child to think as you read stories together or as your child reads independently. You will find that he or she will comprehend and remember stories better—and enjoy reading more.

Sincerely,

Estimada familia de _____,

Nuestra clase ha comenzado a leer cuentos en un libro titulado **Steck-Vaughn Think-Alongs™: Comprehending As You Read.** El libro utiliza un enfoque a la lectura llamado "thinking along" (pensar mientras lee). Su niño/a contestará preguntas y va a dibujar y escribir respuestas mientras la clase lee una variedad de cuentos. Este proceso ayudará a su niño/a a entender y recordar lo que lea.

Usted puede ayudar a su niño/a de muchas maneras. Hágale preguntas sobre los cuentos y de lo que él/ella se siente acerca de los trabajos de dibujar y escribir. Pídale cómo se acostumbra a pensar cuando esté leyendo. Es bien importante que lea con su niño/a, parándose mientras están leyendo para comentar el cuento. Hágale preguntas como, "¿Qué acaba de pasar?" y "¿Qué piensas que ocurrirá?" para reforzar los habilidades de pensar de su niño/a.

Anime a su niño/a a pensar mientras están leyendo cuentos juntos, o cuando lea sólo. Se dará cuenta de que él/ella comprenderá y recordará mejor los cuentos—y disfrutará mejor la lectura.

Atentamente,

Name _____ Date _____

Thinking About Thinking Along

How do you feel about thinking along?
Color the face that shows how you feel.

1. I can draw and write in the boxes when I read.

yes

no

2. Drawing and writing in the boxes makes reading fun.

yes

no

3. Drawing and writing in the boxes helps me think about what I read.

yes

no

4. Drawing and writing in the boxes helps me remember what I read.

yes

no

5. Draw a picture of yourself drawing and writing in the boxes when
you read.

Student _____ Date _____

Checklist for Assessing Thinking Along

	RATING			
Not at all				**All the time**
1	**2**	**3**	**4**	**5**

How is thinking along working with this student?

1. Is the student able to draw or write in the boxes?   **1**   **2**   **3**   **4**   **5**

2. Does the student discuss what he or she drew or wrote in the boxes?   **1**   **2**   **3**   **4**   **5**

3. Can the student support what he or she drew or wrote?   **1**   **2**   **3**   **4**   **5**

4. Does the student use a variety of reading comprehension strategies?   **1**   **2**   **3**   **4**   **5**

5. Does the student seem to understand and remember the story?   **1**   **2**   **3**   **4**   **5**

6. Does the student pay more attention now when a story is read aloud or when he or she is reading?   **1**   **2**   **3**   **4**   **5**

7. Does the student apply thinking along to other types of reading?   **1**   **2**   **3**   **4**   **5**

8. Does the student ask more questions when text from other subject areas is read aloud and when reading in other subject areas?   **1**   **2**   **3**   **4**   **5**

9. Does the student discuss more about what has been read in other subject areas?   **1**   **2**   **3**   **4**   **5**

10. Does the student apply reading comprehension strategies in other subject areas?   **1**   **2**   **3**   **4**   **5**

Scope and Sequence

Strategy	Level					
	A	B	C	D	E	F
Retell by drawing pictures	x	x	x	x	x	x
Connect personal experiences	x	x	x	x	x	x
Identify the main idea	x	x	x	x	x	x
Make predictions	x	x	x	x	x	x
Visualize		x	x	x	x	x
Generate questions		x	x	x	x	x
Identify main ideas and details		x	x	x	x	x
Recognize sequence		x	x	x	x	x
Use background knowledge			x	x	x	x
Compare and contrast			x	x	x	x
Make and revise predictions			x	x	x	x
Distinguish between fantasy and reality			x	x	x	x
Identify cause and effect				x	x	x
Summarize				x	x	x
Identify author's purpose				x	x	x
Draw conclusions					x	x
Evaluate and express opinions					x	x
Identify and interpret meaning of figurative language					x	x
Analyze story elements						x
Identify and analyze problems and solutions						x
Evaluate and interpret author's style and technique						x

Strategy Definitions

Level A

Retell by drawing pictures: Students listen to or read a story and then draw one or more pictures to retell the story.

Connect personal experiences: Students recognize similarities between themselves and their lives and the characters and events in the selections they listen to or read independently.

Identify the main idea: Students express the main idea of a selection either in words or in pictures.

Make predictions: Students speculate about what will happen next in a story.

Level B

Visualize: Students try to picture in their heads what they are reading or listening to in a selection.

Generate questions: Students question events, characters, and details as they read.

Identify main ideas and details: Students determine both explicit and implicit main ideas of a selection. They identify details that support the main idea.

Recognize sequence: Students recall events in a selection in the order in which they occur. They also predict what will happen next or what happened prior to the events described in the selection.

Level C

Use background knowledge: Students use what they already know to interpret the ideas in narrative and expository selections.

Compare and contrast: Students compare relationships between events, objects, or characters to see how they are alike and different.

Make and revise predictions: Students speculate about what will happen next in a narrative or expository selection. They confirm or change their predictions based on subsequent information.

Distinguish between fantasy and reality: Students recognize the difference between what could be real and what could not be real.

Level D

Identify cause and effect: Students identify why something happened (cause) and the consequence of an event or action (effect).

Summarize: Students use textual and typographical clues to recognize the organization of expository text. They use the text organization to summarize the selection.

Identify author's purpose: Students understand an author's purpose in writing a particular story or article. They also are able to identify writing for a specific purpose such as to inform, explain, or entertain.

Level E

Draw conclusions: Students use the information provided in a selection to form a conclusion or make inferences about the topic of the selection.

Evaluate and express opinion: Students develop opinions about the subject or content of a selection or evaluate the opinions expressed by the author or character in a selection.

Identify and interpret meaning of figurative language: Students recognize vivid and colorful language that helps to set the mood of a selection or conveys feelings. They interpret the meaning of figurative language.

Level F

Analyze story elements: Students identify and analyze the characters, setting, theme, or plot in a story.

Identify and analyze problems and solutions: Students identify a problem that is stated or implied in a selection and evaluate the solutions presented in the selection.

Evaluate and interpret author's style and technique: Students determine why an author may have written a selection and how the author's writing style and technique makes the selection interesting or unusual.

Annotated Student Pages for

Steck-Vaughn Think-Alongs:
Comprehending As You Read

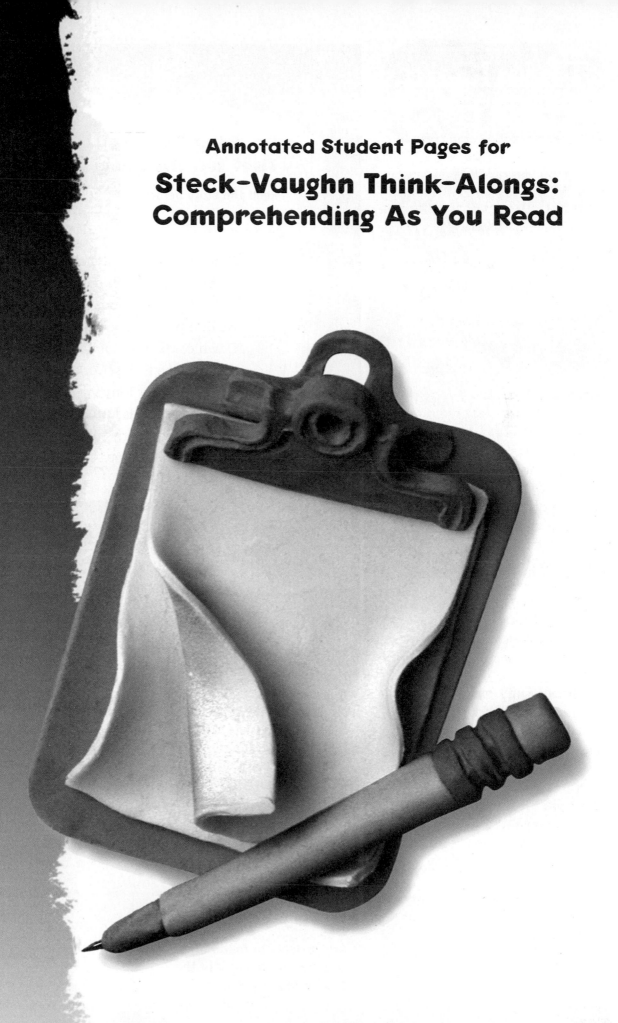

Drawing Pictures That Tell the Story

Retelling by Drawing Pictures

Readers use their imaginations to create mental pictures as they read. The illustrations in beginning reading books assist students in this visualization process and facilitate reading comprehension. One of the best ways to encourage beginning readers to actively engage with a story is to have them retell the story by drawing pictures. The activities in this unit will help students apply this strategy as the stories are read aloud to them. This strategy will help them better understand and enjoy what they read.

Thinking About

Drawing Pictures That Tell the Story

Read the story below.

A big dog ran into the classroom.
He bumped the fish bowl.
It crashed to the floor.
He bumped the bookcase.
Down came a pile of books.
"Whose dog is this?" asked the teacher.
The dog ran to Tony's desk.
He jumped in his lap.
"It's my dog," Tony said.
"I'll take him home."

4

Introducing the Strategy

Ask students to tell about something that happened in class today. Perhaps they visited the school library, they participated in an art project, or a visitor came to the classroom. Ask students what they would draw if they were trying to tell someone about this event. Call on children to tell what they would show in their drawings.

Applying the Strategy

Ask students to follow along as you read the story in the pupil book, or ask them to listen carefully as you read the story if they are not yet able to follow along with the words. Encourage them to visualize, or picture in their heads, the events that occur in the story. When you have finished reading, ask students what happened in the story. Encourage students to describe how the classroom might have looked after the dog ran through it.

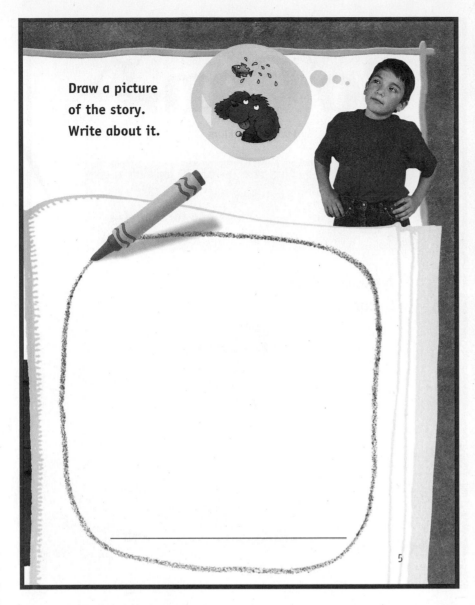

Draw a picture
of the story.
Write about it.

5

Discussing the Strategy

Have students draw a picture about something that happened in the story. Ask for volunteers to share their drawings with the class. Ask them to explain what part of the story their drawings show. Explain that they will draw pictures about the stories you will read in this unit. Tell them that drawing pictures will help them understand what happens in each story.

Presenting the Stories

Many of your beginning readers may not be able to read or follow along as you are reading the stories in this unit aloud. If this is the case, encourage students to listen carefully as you read without having them follow along with the words. Be sure to call attention to the pictures that accompany the text, and help students keep their books open to the appropriate pages as you read the story to them.

In this unit, suggested think-along questions are provided at intervals throughout each story in the teacher's edition.

You are encouraged to discuss these, or your own questions, with students as you read to enhance student comprehension. Students are asked to draw their responses to stories on the "Time to Write" activity pages that appear at the end of each story in the pupil's edition.

So Can I

Strategy Focus

Retelling by drawing a picture.

Story at a Glance

This story tells what both animals and children can do.

Vocabulary

You may want to introduce the following words to your students:

monkey   squirrel
rabbit   help

Getting Students Started

- **Introducing the Story**

Introduce the story by asking students to think about things that a cat or dog might do, such as sleeping, eating, and jumping. Ask students if they can do these things, too. Ask students to talk about what a goldfish or a parrot can do, such as swimming or flying. Ask students if they can do either of these. Explain to them that they are going to hear a story that tells about what animals and children can do.

- **Purpose for Reading**

Students listen to learn what animals and children can both do.

So Can I

By Margery Facklam

This story is about animals and what they do.
What can you do that animals can do?

A fish can swim.
So can I.

6

A monkey can swing.

So can I.

Strategy Tip

Tell students that retelling the story out loud and in a drawing will help them think about the story.

Think-Along Question 1

After you have read pages 6–7 aloud, ask, "What does the story tell you about something an animal can do that you can do, too?"

Possible Responses

Fish can swim.
Most students will be able to summarize by telling about either the fish or the monkey. Ask students, "Can you swim, too?"

My dog barks at birds.
First-grade students who are eager to tell about their own pets may miss the point of the question. Tell them that you like to hear about their pets, but ask if they can remember something an animal in the story can do.

I don't know how to swim.
This response demonstrates that the student understands the story and has thought about the question. Ask, "Do you know people who can swim? What animal in the story can swim?"

A dog can dig.

So can I.

8

A horse can run.

So can I.

9

Think-Along Question 2

After you have read pages 8–9 aloud, say, "The story says that a horse and a person can run. What do you think the story is going to say next?"

Possible Responses

So can I!

I can do it too.

The student has not recognized the pattern in the story. Ask, "Can you think of an animal that will be next?"

It will tell about another animal.

This student understands the pattern in the story. Ask, "What animals do you think we will learn about?"

Meeting Individual Needs

Find other predictable stories in the school library to read to students, such as *Brown Bear, Brown Bear, What Do You See?* by Bill Martin, Jr. Encourage students to draw pictures that illustrate an idea presented in the story.

A frog can jump.

So can I.

11

Think-Along Question 3

After you have read pages 10–11 aloud, ask, "What animals did we just read about that can do something that you can do, too?"

. . . .

Possible Responses

Kangaroos can jump and hop.
This student has been thinking about the story and is understanding what different animals can do. Say, "You thought about an animal that can jump and hop. What animals does the *story* say can hop and jump?"

[Several students may demonstrate their responses by hopping and jumping.]
If students respond by hopping and jumping, say,

"We seem to have several hoppers and jumpers. Who can tell which animals in the story can hop and jump?"

Rabbits and frogs—toads can too.
The student's response shows an understanding of the main idea on this page by relating it to background knowledge.

A squirrel can climb.

So can I.

A bear can hug.

So can I.

13

Think-Along Question 4

After you have read pages 12–13 aloud, ask, "What did the story say that bears and squirrels can do?"

Possible Responses

Squirrels climb and bears hug. I wouldn't want to be hugged by a bear.

This student is able to retell what has been read and is also stating an opinion based on the story and background knowledge of bears. Ask, "Why wouldn't you want to be hugged by a bear?"

I can climb and I hug my teddy bear.

The student demonstrates comprehension of the story by relating it to personal experience.

Squirrels made a nest in our attic.

This student is connecting a personal experience to the story. Ask, "Do you think the squirrels who made the nest could climb?"

After Reading

- Ask students to think of a favorite story that they have heard or read, or a TV show or movie that they have seen recently. Tell students to draw pictures to describe the characters or events in the story, TV show, or movie.
- Tell students to think of something special they can do. Have them draw a picture that shows them participating in this activity. Ask students to share their pictures with the class. Have students ask questions and try to guess what is shown in each of their classmate's pictures.

A bird can fly.
So can I.
But I need some help!

14

Think-Along Question 5

After you have read this page aloud, ask, "What does the story say about what you can do?"

....

Possible Responses

People can't fly but an airplane can take them up.
The student's response shows an understanding of the story and strong critical thinking skills. Ask, "What do you think it would be like to fly with your own wings?"

I wish that I could fly like a bird.
This student is thinking about the story, but is not directly addressing the

question. Say, "It would be fun to fly with your own wings. Can you fly with some help?"

How could a person fly?
This is a thoughtful question that reflects good reading comprehension and strong critical thinking skills. Ask, "Do people ever fly from one place to another? How do they do that?"

Time to Write!

Draw a picture about the story.
Write about your picture.

15

Making Connections

Activity Links

- Have students choose an animal and act out something the animal can do. Let the "actor" choose students to guess what it is they are doing.
- Tell the students you are going to name an animal and tell something the animal can do, such as, "A frog can hop." Ask students to act out the animal and action you have named.
- Have students tell something they can do and name an animal that can do that same thing.
- Bring a picture book of animals to class and discuss with students what different animals can do (choose animals that are not included in the selection). Ask students if they can do these things, too.

Reading Links

You might want to include these books in a discussion of what animals and people can do:

- *Polar Bear, Polar Bear, What Do You Hear?* by Bill Martin, Jr. (Henry Holt and Co., 1997).
- *Big Red Barn* by Margaret Wise Brown (Harpercollins Juvenile Books, 1989).
- *Where Does the Brown Bear Go?* by Nicki Weiss (Greenwillow, 1989).

Writing

Ask students to follow along at the top of page 15 as you read the directions aloud. Ask them to draw a picture of some of the animals that you read about. Tell them that their drawings can show the animals doing something that the students can do, and they can show students in the picture doing these things, too. Point out that there is a place at the bottom of the page for them to write a caption for their picture.

Walk around the room and encourage students as they are drawing. This is a good opportunity for you to work individually with your students to learn how many are able to tell about the story with drawings. You can learn more about their ideas if you occasionally ask them to explain their drawings or if you write a dictated response for them.

Sharing

Ask students to share their pictures with other students and describe what they have drawn. Encourage students to tell if their picture shows an animal from the story doing something that they can do, too.

15

There Is a Town

Strategy Focus

Retelling by drawing a picture.

Story at a Glance

During her birthday party, a girl opens a box that came in a dollhouse that came in a bigger box, in a room, in a house, on a street, in a town.

Vocabulary

You may want to introduce the following words to your students:

town	*words*
street	*goes*
box	

Getting Students Started

- **Introducing the Selection**

  Ask students to tell about the street where they live. Encourage them to describe the houses or apartments. Ask them to imagine how some of the rooms look in the houses or apartments on their street.

- **Purpose for Reading**

  Students listen to learn what happens in the room in the house.

There Is a Town

By Gail Herman

This story tells about a room—in a house—on a street—in a town. What happens in the room in the house?

There is a town.
And in this town,
there is a street.

16

And on this street,
there is a house.
And in this house,
there is a room.
And in this room,
there is a box.

Strategy Tip

Tell students that telling about a story as it is being read, and drawing pictures about the story when it is over, will help them remember and enjoy the story.

17

Think-Along Question 1

After you have read pages 16–17 aloud, ask, "What do you think is in the box?"

Possible Responses

It's a birthday present.
Most students' responses will be similar to this one. Students will use the picture clues to talk about the gift box. Emphasize the picture clues by asking, "What makes you think it is a birthday present?"

A big teddy bear
This student is making a reasonable prediction. Encourage the student to visualize by asking, "What do you think the teddy bear looks like?"

A set of trains
This student is also making a reasonable prediction about the gift in the box. Ask, "What makes you think it is a set of trains?"

And in this box,
there is a house.
And in this house,
there is a room.
And in this room,
there is a box.

18

Think-Along Question 2

After you have read page 18 aloud, ask, "What do you think is in <u>this</u> box?"

. . . .

Possible Responses

It's another present!
This student has clearly comprehended the pattern in the story. Ask, "What do you see in the picture that makes you think there is another present in the box?"

There's going to be a littler house.
This student is using the repeating pattern in the story to predict what is in the box. Ask, "Why do you think there is a littler house?"

There's a present on the table in the picture.
This response indicates the student has used the picture clues and pattern clues in the story to tell about the box. To further emphasize the picture clues ask, "What do you think the present is?"

And in this box,
there is a cake.
And on this cake,
there are some words.

19

Think-Along Question 3

After you have read page 19 aloud, ask, "What do you think the words on the cake say?"

....

Possible Responses

It's a birthday cake.
This student either is reading the words on the cake or is predicting what the words say based on story context. To encourage the student to think about additional details in the picture, ask, "What in the picture makes you think it is a birthday cake?"

I think that's a fake cake.
This response indicates a close examination of the picture clues. Ask, "What makes you say that it is not a real cake?"

That cake says "Happy Birthday Maria."
This student is making a personal connection with the text by placing herself in the story and pretending it is her birthday cake. Ask, "Why do you think the cake says 'Happy Birthday Maria'?"

Words on the cake,
cake in the box,
box in the room,
room in the house,
house in the box,
box in the room,

For students who are acquiring English, have them say key words from the story in their first language, including *town, street, house, room,* and *box*. Have them use pictures in the story as references.

20

room in the house,
house on the street,

21

Read the first page of the story and have students imagine they are looking at a street in their neighborhood. Ask them to draw a picture of the street. Encourage them to show people in their drawing.

After Reading

- Read aloud a picture book that has a repeating pattern. After reading the story aloud, ask students to retell the story based on the pattern and pictures. You may want to use one of the following picture books that has a repeating pattern:
  - *I Went Walking* by Sue Williams (Red Wagon, 1996).
  - *Are You My Mother?* By P.D. Eastman (Random House, 1987).
  - *Mushroom in the Rain* by Mirra Ginsburg (Aladdin, 1997).
  - *Rosie's Walk* by Pat Hutchins (Macmillan, 1983).

- Tell students to look out the window and think about the many things they see. Then ask them to tell what they saw when they looked out the window. Write a list of what students saw on the chalkboard. Next have students draw a picture of something they saw when they looked out the window.

street in the town—
that goes to sleep.

22

Think-Along Question 4

After you have read pages 20–22 aloud, ask, "How does the story end?"

Possible Responses

They went home and the whole town went to sleep.
  This response uses the picture clue that shows that there is no activity in the town. Ask, "How do you know that the whole town went to sleep?"

Everybody went to sleep. Everyone is happy.
  By adding, "Everyone is happy," this student takes the simple repetitive story and gives it a happy ending. This student is likely using background knowledge about other stories that end with, "And they lived happily ever after." Ask, "What makes you think everyone is happy?"

She put the new house on the table in her room.
  This student uses the picture clue that shows the doll-house on the table next to the girl's bed. Ask, "Why do you think she put the new house there?"

Time to Write!

Draw a picture about the story.
Write about your picture.

23

Making Connections

Activity Links

- Have students play a game called "Guess What Is in the Box." One student tells a clue about something that could be inside a box. After the student tells the clue, the other students guess what could be in the box. The students take turns making up clues about something that could be in a box.

- Have students make up dialogue for the family looking at the box. Call attention to the picture clues, especially the facial expressions, to think about what the people might be saying. To help students create dialogue, ask, "What might the mother say?" "What might the little brother say?" "What might the girl say?" and "What might her friends say?"

- Have students tell ways that the town, street, house, and room in the story are alike and different from their town, street, house, and room.

Reading Links

- *Citybook* by Shelley Rotner and Ken Kreisler (Orchard Books, 1994).
- *My Street* by Rebecca Treays (EDC Publications, 1999).
- *My Town* by Rebecca Treays (EDC Publications, 1998).

Writing

Ask students to follow along at the top of page 23 as you read the directions aloud. Ask them to draw a picture of something that happened in the story. Tell them that their drawings can show the town, the house, the room, the box, or any other part of the story. Point out that there is a place at the bottom of the page for them to write a caption for their picture.

Walk around the room and encourage students as they are drawing. This is a good opportunity for you to work individually with students to learn how many are able to tell about the story with drawings. You can learn more about their ideas if you occasionally ask them to explain their drawings or if you write a dictated response for them.

Sharing

Ask students to share their pictures with classmates and tell what they have drawn. Ask them to tell other things that happened in the story.

Bears, Bears, and More Bears

Strategy Focus

Retelling by drawing a picture.

Story at a Glance

This story tells about different kinds of bears. It tells what colors they are, what they can do, and what they eat.

Vocabulary

You may want to introduce the following words to your students:
bears
berries
bamboo

Getting Students Started

• Introducing the Selection

Introduce the story by asking students if they have ever seen a live bear. Ask them to tell where they saw the bear, what it looked like, and what it was doing. Then ask if they have seen bears on TV or in books. Ask them to describe these bears. Tell them that they are going to hear a story about all kinds of bears.

• Purpose for Reading

Students listen to learn something new about bears so they can draw a picture showing what they learned.

Bears, Bears, and More Bears

By Jackie Morris

Let's Read

This story tells about all different kinds of bears.
What kinds of bears do you like?

There are little bears.

24

There are big bears.

25

Strategy Tip

Tell students that retelling a story out loud and drawing pictures about a story will help them think about it.

Think-Along Question 1

After you have read pages 24–25 aloud, ask, "What did you learn about how bears look?"

....

Possible Responses

There are bear cubs.
The student has recognized the little bears from the picture. Ask, "What size are bear cubs?"

Some bears are huge—and they can chase people.
In this response the student is using background knowledge to show an understanding of the story. Ask, "Where did you learn so much about bears?"

How big can a bear be?
This response reflects a good understanding of the story. Tell this student that bears can be bigger than a large adult and as small as a small dog.

25

Bears can be black.

Bears can be brown.

Bears can even be white.

26

Think-Along Question 2

After you have read this page aloud, ask, "What did you find out about bears on this page?"

· ·

Possible Responses

I saw a polar bear.
This student has recognized the polar bear from the story picture. Ask what the polar bear looks like. Ask the student to tell about the color, size, and other physical characteristics of the polar bear.

My dad said black bears are very dangerous.
In this response the student uses background knowledge to relate to the story. Ask,

"Did you learn about other kinds of bears on this page?"

Bears are all different colors. I wonder how many colors they can be.
In this response, the student has made a good observation and has asked a question that reflects strong critical thinking skills. Encourage this student to count how many different colors are shown.

Most bears sleep all winter.

27

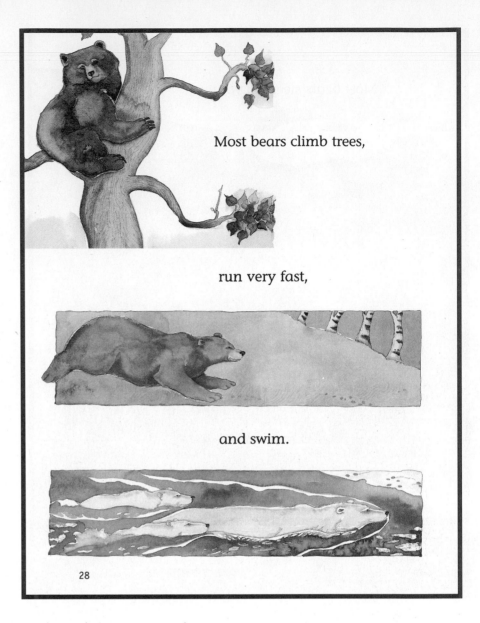

Most bears climb trees,

run very fast,

and swim.

28

Think-Along Question 3

After you have read pages 27–28 aloud, ask, "What did you learn about bears?"

· ·

Possible Responses

Bears can swim.
This student has listened and learned something new about bears. Ask, "How do you think bears look when they swim?"

Bears can do lots of things. I saw bears on TV ride a bicycle.
This student is using background knowledge to relate to the reading. To ensure that the student understands

the reading, ask, "What were some of the things the bears in this story did?"

I'm going to draw bears climbing trees. I didn't know they could do that.
This student has discussed something he or she learned from the story and is motivated to draw the image. Ask, "What will you draw in your picture?"

Some bears eat berries.

Some bears eat fish.

29

Think-Along Question 4

After you have read this page aloud, ask, "What did you find out about bears on this page?"

· ·

Possible Responses

Bears eat fish.
By this point in the story students should be listening and repeating the ideas from the story. To reinforce the strategy of visualization, ask this student to tell you how bears look when they catch and eat fish.

Bears run fast.
In this response the student has repeated something from earlier in the text that he or she has learned. Ask, "Why do you think bears might run?"

What kind of berries? Strawberries?
This student is looking for information beyond what the text provides, which indicates strong critical thinking skills. He or she is also using background knowledge of berries to question and understand the reading.

Ask students acquiring English to describe bears in their first language. They may have special names for panda bears, black bears, and polar bears. They may even be able to tell how a bear growls in their language. Many times the sounds that animals make are represented differently in different languages.

Some bears eat bamboo.

30

Some bears aren't real bears at all.

Think-Along Question 5

After you have read pages 30–31 aloud, ask, "What did you learn about bears?"

....

Possible Responses

I don't understand how a bear can't be a bear.

This response reflects strong critical thinking skills. Explain that a koala is not really a bear, but because it looks like a bear many people think of it as a bear (like the kangaroo, the koala is actually a marsupial).

There are all kinds of bears.

This response indicates that the student is learning that bears come in a variety of sizes and colors. Ask, "Did you know there were so many kinds of bears before we read this story?"

What is bamboo?

When students express confusion about a new word, encourage them to define the word from the story context and from picture clues. After helping this student learn what bamboo is, ask, "What does the story say bears do with bamboo?"

After Reading

- Ask students to think about coming to school this morning—walking, riding in a car, or riding on the school bus. Tell students to think of something that was different or unusual that they saw on the way to school. First, ask the students to tell what they saw. Then, ask students to draw a picture of what they saw. Encourage students to write a caption for their pictures.

- Model for the students how you use a story's pictures to help understand the story. Use a new or familiar story as an example. As you are showing the pictures to the class, describe how you look at and think about the pictures. For example, you might say:

When I read, I look at the pictures to help me understand what I am reading. The pictures help me figure out what the words mean. Sometimes the pictures show things that the words do not say. Looking at the pictures helps me understand and enjoy the story.

Point to pictures in the story that tell you more about the story or hint at upcoming events in the story.

There are lots of bears in the world.

But the best bear is your bear.

32

Think-Along Question 6

After you have read this page aloud, ask, "What did you learn about bears on this page?"

Possible Responses

It's not a real bear.
This response shows that the student understands the reading. Ask, "Do you have a teddy bear that looks like the teddy bear in the picture?"

It's a teddy bear.
This student has correctly identified the bear that is described in this section of the reading. Ask, "Why do you think a teddy bear

might be someone's favorite bear?"

Some bears aren't even real.
This response reveals an understanding of the main idea of the story—that there are many kinds of bears. Ask, "How does the teddy bear in the picture look like a real bear?"

Time to Write!

What did you find out about bears?
Draw a picture.
Write about your picture.

33

Writing

Ask students to follow along at the top of page 33 as you read the directions aloud. Tell students to draw a picture that shows something that they learned about bears. Point out that there is a place to write at the bottom of the page so that they can label their picture if they would like.

Walk around the room and encourage students as they are drawing. This is a good opportunity for you to work individually with your students to learn how many are able to describe the story by drawing pictures. You can

learn more about their ideas if you occasionally ask them to explain their drawings. Some students will add things that are not in the story. This is appropriate, but encourage them to include something new they learned about bears from the story.

Sharing

Ask students to share their drawings by showing them to other students and explaining what they learned about bears. Alternatively, students may want to have other students guess what the bears in their drawings are doing.

Making Connections

Activity Links

- Have students make collages or a poster featuring bears. Have students use images that they find in old magazines or books to create their collages or posters. Encourage students to find pictures of bears doing different activities.
- Ask students to draw a picture of their favorite animal. Encourage them to show something these animals can do in their drawings.
- Have students act out some of the activities that the bears in this story do. For example, ask students to take turns acting out bears eating berries, swimming, running, or climbing trees, and have other students guess what action is being portrayed.

Reading Links

You might want to include these books in a discussion about bears:

- *Little Polar Bear Finds a Friend* by Hans de Beer (North South Books, 1996).
- *Bear Day* by Cynthia Rylant (Harcourt Brace, 1998).
- *Bears: Polar Bears, Black Bears and Grizzly Bears* by Deborah Hodge (Kids Can Press, 1997).

Thinking About...

What Happened to You

Thinking About

What Happened to You

Have you ever gone shopping?
Read the story below.

The Three Bears went shopping.
Baby Bear got black boots like Papa Bear's.
Mama Bear got a new pot for oatmeal.
Papa Bear said, "I need a new hat to keep the sun out of my eyes."
He bought a hat made out of straw.
Baby Bear said, "Let's buy something for Grandma Bear."
They looked in all the stores.
"It's not easy to find something for Grandma Bear," said Baby Bear.

34

Connecting Personal Experiences

One of the most important reading strategies is relating what you read to personal experiences. Students often see themselves doing what story characters do, but sometimes they need encouragement to relate story events to their own lives. This strategy can be developed by asking students questions as stories are being read. These types of think-along questions will help students relate their personal experiences to characters, events, and places presented in a variety of stories. The activities in this unit will help students apply the strategy of connecting stories to personal experiences. This strategy will help them to better understand and remember what they read.

Introducing the Strategy

Ask students to think about a familiar story such as "Goldilocks and the Three Bears." Encourage students to describe story events by asking specific questions such as the following:
- *Who are the Three Bears?*
- *Where do they live?*
- *Who is Goldilocks?*
- *What does Goldilocks do at the bears' house?*
- *How does the story end?*

Ask students what they would draw if they were trying to show what happens in "Goldilocks and the Three Bears."

Applying the Strategy

Tell students that you are going to read another story about the Three Bears. Ask students to follow along as you read the story in the pupil book, or ask them to listen carefully as you read the story if they are not yet able to follow along with the words. Tell them to think about connecting what happens in the story to things they have done.

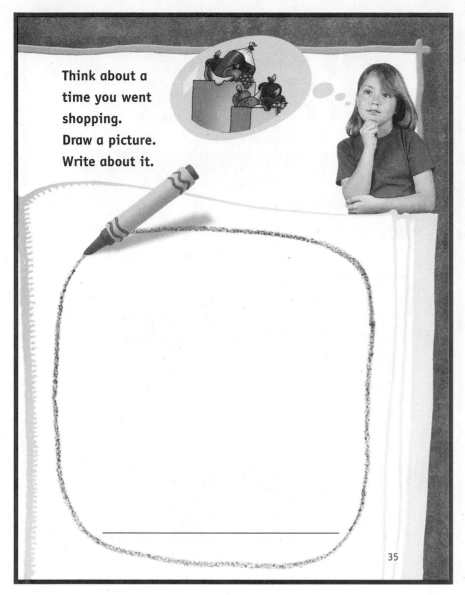

Think about a
time you went
shopping.
Draw a picture.
Write about it.

35

When you have finished reading, ask students what happened in the story. Encourage them to relate events in the story to personal experiences. Ask questions such as the following:

- *Do you go shopping?*
- *What kinds of stores do you visit?*
- *What kinds of things did your family buy the last time you went shopping?*

Next, ask students to draw a picture in which they are shopping with a family member or friend. Ask for volunteers to share their drawings with the class. Ask them to explain who is in the drawing, where they are shopping, and what the objects are that appear in their drawings. Tell them that thinking about things they have done will help them understand what happens in a story.

Presenting the Stories

Many of your beginning readers may not be able to read or follow along as you are reading the stories in this unit aloud. If this is the case, encourage students to listen carefully as you read without having them follow along with the words. Be sure to call attention to the pictures that accompany the text, and help students keep their books open to the appropriate pages as you read.

In this unit, suggested questions to ask students are provided at intervals throughout each story in the teacher's edition. You are encouraged to discuss these, or your own questions, with students as you read to enhance student comprehension. Students are asked to draw their responses to stories on the "Time to Write" activity pages that appear at the end of each story in the pupil's edition.

My Sister Is My Friend

Strategy Focus

Using personal experiences to think about a story.

Story at a Glance

A big sister helps her little brother find missing belongings, making the boy thankful that his sister is his friend.

Vocabulary

You may want to introduce the following words to your students:
sister
friend

Getting Students Started

- **Introducing the Selection**

Introduce the story by asking students if they have older brothers or sisters. Ask students to talk about times when their sister or brother helped them do something. Encourage students to talk about other activities they like to with their siblings. Tell students that they are going to read a story in which a little brother is helped by his older sister and is glad that his sister is his friend.

- **Purpose for Reading**

Students listen to find out what the big sister helps her little brother do.

My Sister Is My Friend

By Hannah Markley

Let's Read

This story is about a little boy and his big sister.
She helps him.
How do older people help you?

My sister finds my socks.

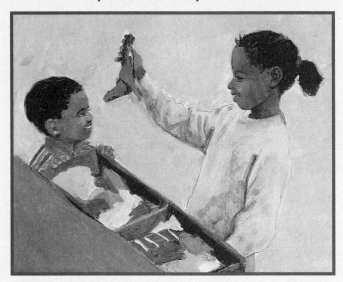

36

My sister finds my shoes.

My sister finds my book.

37

Think-Along Question 1

After you have read pages 36–37 aloud, ask, "What is something that somebody helped you find?"

. . . .

Possible Responses

A ball

Encourage the student to elaborate on this response by asking, "Who helped you? Where did you find the ball?"

Sometimes I look for my shoes but I can't find them.

This student is connecting personal experience to the story, but has not addressed the question. Ask, "Who helps you find your shoes when you can't find them?"

I helped my mom find the right box of cereal at the grocery store.

This student is using personal experience to relate to the story. Encourage the student to more directly address the question by saying, "You help your mom find things. Is there something that she helps you find?"

My sister finds my coat.

38

My sister finds my snake.

 **ESOL**

Have students acquiring English draw pictures of different family members and write the names of each of these family members beneath their pictures. Ask students to include terms such as *mother, father, sister, brother,* or *grandma* under the names of these individuals, if possible. The book *Family Pictures* by Carmen Lomas Garza (Children's Book Press, 1990), which is written in English and Spanish, may be helpful.

After Reading

- Have students write name poems about someone in their family. Each line of the name poem should start with a letter of the family member's name. Each line should describe something that the student enjoys doing with that family member or something special that the student likes about the family member. For example, if a student chooses to write about his or her father, the poem might be as follows:

  - **D**rives me to school every day

  - **A**lways reads to me

  - **D**rinks milkshakes with me

- The story "My Sister Is My Friend" is about friendship. Have students read other books about friends, such as the following:

  - *My Best Friend* by Pat Hutchins (Greenwillow, 1993).

  - *Together* by George Ella Lyon (Orchard Books, 1989).

  After students have read one of these books, ask them to think about a good friend. Ask students, "What do you enjoy doing with your friend?" Then, have students draw a picture showing something that they like to do with their friend. Encourage students to write captions for their pictures.

I'm glad my sister is my friend.

40

Think-Along Question 2

After you have have read pages 38–40 aloud, ask, "Do you have a friend who has helped you?"

. . . .

Possible Responses

Julio helped me when I couldn't find my sweatshirt.
The student uses personal experience to answer the question. Ask, "Is there a time when you helped Julio find something?"

Mommy helped me when I lost my baseball mitt.
As in the previous response, this student uses personal experience to answer the question.

My baby sister always wants me to play with her, so I do.
It is not clear from this response whether or not the student has understood the question. Ask, "Do you ever help your baby sister when you are playing with her? Does she ever help you?"

Who helps you?
Draw a picture.
Write about your picture.

41

Writing

Ask students to follow along at the top of page 41 as you read the directions aloud. Tell them that they will draw a picture showing how someone helps them. The person might be an older brother or sister, a cousin, or their mothers or fathers. Encourage students to write about their picture at the bottom of the page.

Walk around the room and encourage students as they are drawing. This is a good opportunity for you to work individually with students to learn how many are able to connect the story to personal experiences by drawing pictures. You can learn more about their ideas if you occasionally ask them to explain their drawings, or by writing a dictated caption for them.

Sharing

Organize students into pairs. Ask them to act out how the person in their drawing helped them.

Making Connections

Activity Links

• Ask students to think of things that they can do to help keep the classroom tidy: pick up papers from the floor, wash paint brushes, water plants, put blocks away, etc. Ask them to talk about how helping keep the classroom tidy is important.

• Motivate students to be classroom helpers by having them make "Helping Hands" by tracing their hands and writing their names on them. After you have made a board that lists the duties to be done by the classroom helpers, students can put their "Helping Hands" next to the task they will be doing that week.

• Ask students to keep a list for one week of the ways that they help people in their families, and the ways that family members help them. Encourage students to write or draw about these helping experiences.

Reading Links

You might want to include these books in a discussion of families and helping:

• *We Are Best Friends* by Aliki (Mulberry Books, 1982).

• *Loving* by Ann Morris (Lothrop, Lee & Shepard, 1990).

• *Chicken Sunday* (Philomel, 1992) and *The Keeping Quilt* (Simon & Schuster, 1982) by Patricia Polacco.

Strategy Focus

Using personal experiences to think about a story.

Story at a Glance

Students are encouraged to identify different wheeled objects presented throughout the book.

Vocabulary

You may want to introduce the following words to your students:
wheels
spare

Getting Students Started

• Introducing the Selection

Ask students to list all the things they can think of that have wheels. Write the list on the board. Ask students to tell you how many wheels are attached to each of the objects they named. Write these numbers next to each item in the list. Tell students that they are going to hear a story about things that have wheels.

• Purpose for Reading

Students listen to find out if they have ridden any of the objects with wheels that are discussed in the story.

All Kinds of Wheels

By Stephanie Handwerker

This story is about things that have wheels.
What do you ride that has wheels?

I have one large wheel.
You can ride me at the fair.

42

I have two wheels.
You can ride me anywhere.

43

Think-Along Question 1

After you have read the first two pages aloud, ask, "What do you have that has one wheel or two wheels?"

Possible Responses

My bicycle has 2 big wheels and 2 little wheels.

The student's response connects personal experience to the story. Ask, "Can you tell me more about your bicycle?"

After 2 comes 3.

This response shows that the student understands the counting structure of the story. Redirect the student to answer the question by asking, "Do you have anything that has two wheels?"

I rode one of those with Dad at the fair.

This student is relating personal experience to the story. Encourage the student to clarify his or her response by asking, "What did you ride with your dad? A Ferris wheel? What was it like?"

I have three wheels.
I fly down to the ground.

44

I have four wheels.
Pull me to turn around.

45

I have five wheels.
Count my spare tire, too.

Think-Along Question 2

After you have read pages 44–46 aloud, ask, "Do the things in these pictures look like anything that your family has?"

....

Possible Responses

My brother's bike has three wheels.

This student is probably refering to a tricycle. Encourage the student to clarify his or her response by asking, "Can you tell me more about what your brother has with three wheels? Does he ride it? Is it like a bicycle?"

We went to Grandma's house in an airplane.

The student's response connects personal experience to the story. Ask, "Did the airplane look like the one in the picture, or was it bigger? What did you think about riding in the airplane?"

Red wagon!

This response could use elaboration. Ask, "Does someone in your family have a red wagon?"

I have many wheels.
The sound I make is choo-choo.

Have students draw pictures of objects with different numbers of wheels. Then, collect all student drawings. Describe the objects in the drawings before showing the drawings to students and have them guess what you are describing. For example, tell them, "I am red. I have four wheels. I am used to pull things. I have a handle. What am I?" [a wagon]

After Reading

- Present a book without words to students. Ask them to help you "tell" the story as you look at the pictures together. Focus on using the details in the pictures to create a story. You may want to have students work in small groups to tell, or retell, the story. Several possible books without words are the following:

  - *Good Dog Carl* by Alexandra Day (Aladdin, 1997).

  - *Peter Spier's Rain* by Peter Spier (Yearling, 1997).

  - *The Snowman* by Raymond Briggs (Random House, 1989).

  - *Tuesday* by David Wiesner (Clarion, 1991).

- Organize students into small groups and have them think about other objects with wheels that were not described in the story "All Kinds of Wheels." Ask students to draw a picture of one of these objects with wheels. The students can post these pictures on a bulletin board display that is titled, "More Kinds of Wheels."

Here are wheels of every kind.
How many wheels can you find?

48

Think-Along Question 3

After you have read pages 47–48 aloud, ask, "What are some other things that you know that have wheels?"

Possible Responses

Wheelbarrows have one wheel.

This response uses background knowledge to relate to the story. Ask, "What does a wheelbarrow look like? Does someone in your family have a wheelbarrow?"

firetrucks

Encourage the students to elaborate. Ask, "What do firetrucks look like? How many wheels do they have?"

[Note: Many large firetrucks have ten or more wheels.]

Trains go woo-woo not choo-choo.

Although this student has not answered the question, he or she is using personal experience to critically read the text. Ask, "Why do you say that it makes the sound woo-woo? Can you name something else that has wheels?"

Time to Write!

What can you ride that has wheels?
Draw a picture.
Write about your picture.

49

Making Connections

49

Activity Links

- Have students focus on objects that are round. Ask students to bring in round objects or pictures of objects to share with the class. Discuss ways to classify the objects.
- Students can create collages to demonstrate their understanding of the numbers 1 through 10 by using real objects. For example, a student might glue 5 pieces of colored construction paper, 4 paper clips, or 8 grains of rice to a piece of poster board to demonstrate their understanding of these numbers.
- Students can create and solve a math problem. Have them draw several vehicles with wheels, then write the answer to the question, "How many wheels all together?"

Reading Links

You might want to include the following books in a discussion of counting or wheels:

- *Rooster's Off to See the World* (Picture Book Studio, 1974) and *1,2,3 to the Zoo* (Putnam & Grosset, 1991) by Eric Carle.
- *Fish Eyes* by Lois Ehlert (Harcourt Brace, 1990).
- *The Wheels on the Bus* by Maryann Kovalski (Little, Brown, 1987).

Writing

Ask students to follow along at the top of page 49 as you read the directions aloud. Tell students to draw a picture that shows them riding something with wheels. Encourage them to write about their picture at the bottom of the page.

Walk around the room and encourage students as they are drawing. This is a good opportunity for you to work individually with students to learn how many are able to connect the story to personal experience by drawing pictures. You can learn more about their ideas if you occasionally ask them to explain their drawings or if you write a dictated caption for them.

Sharing

Ask students to share their drawings with the class. Have students help collect these drawings to create a bulletin board display about wheels.

Strategy Focus

Using personal experiences to think about a story.

Story at a Glance

As Sam searches for his boots, he recalls how he used them in each season.

Vocabulary

You may want to introduce the following words to your students:

spring   *winter*
summer   *seasons*
autumn

Getting Students Started

- **Introducing the Selection**

Introduce the story by asking students to think about the different seasons of the year: spring, summer, autumn, and winter. Ask them to describe the activities that they do in each season. Have them compare the clothing that they wear in each season.

- **Purpose for Reading**

Students listen to the story to find out what Sam does with his boots during each season.

Sam's Seasons

By Christine Price

Let's Read

This story is about a boy named Sam. He is looking for his boots. Have you ever looked for something?

Sam, where are your boots?
Mom, do I have to find them today?
I don't remember where I left them.

50

Think-Along Question 1

After you have read this page aloud, ask, "Can you tell the class about something you could not find?"

Possible Responses

I lost my brown bear Bubbles.
This student has responded directly to the question. By telling about a personal possession he or she has lost, the student is connecting the story to a personal experience.

I lost my boots too. I was sad because I couldn't find them.
This student is relating the story to his or her personal experience and feelings. Ask, "Do you think Sam is sad?"

Sam should always put them in the closet.
Although this student has not responded to the question asked, he or she is demonstrating an understanding of the story by expressing an opinion.

Sam, please find your boots.

Last spring, I wore them in the rain.
I splashed in the water puddles.

 51

Strategy Tip

Tell students to think about what they have done that the character in the story has done, too. This will help them understand the story.

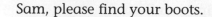

Sam, please find your boots.

Last summer, I wore them to the beach.
I filled them with sand to make a castle.

52

Think-Along Question 2

After you have read pages 51–52 aloud, ask, "What things could you lose in summer?"

Possible Responses

I lost my crayons.

This student is referring to a specific experience. Ask, "Did you lose these during the summer? If not, do you remember what season it was?"

boots

This is a valid response, but it is unclear whether the student has understood the question. Encourage the student to clarify his or her response by asking, "Did you lose your boots in the summer? Can you think of anything else you have lost in the summer?"

You could lose your bucket and shovel.

This response indicates that the student understands the question. Ask, "Have you ever lost a bucket and shovel during the summer?"

Sam, please find your boots.

Last autumn, I wore them in the leaves. I raked the leaves into a pile and jumped in.

 53

 ESOL

Some students may be able to share the names of the seasons in a non-English language. Ask students to draw images of each season and label each picture in English and in their first language. Use the pictures to set up a "Seasons Around the World" display or bulletin board.

Sam, please find your boots.

Last winter, I wore them in the snow.
I used them to help stop my sled.

54

Sam, please find your boots.
They must be somewhere in here.
I know I wore them all four seasons.

But Sam, where are your boots NOW?

55

Think-Along Question 3

After you have read pages 53–55 aloud, ask, "Where do you look for your shoes or your boots when you can't find them?"

Possible Responses

I found my shoes in the closet this morning.

Under the bed.

Both of these responses indicate that the students are using the pictures to answer the question. The first student is also using personal experience.

He looked everywhere in his room. The boots were there somewhere.

This student has not responded to the question. However, the response does indicate that the student is thinking about and understanding the story. Ask, "Where do you look for your shoes when you can't find them?"

After Reading

- Ask students which season of the year they like best: spring, summer, autumn, or winter. Ask them to tell why they like this season. If no student picks a season as a favorite, tell the class some of the reasons why you think that season is special. Encourage students to describe how each season is special where you live, as well as in other parts of the country that they might be familiar with. Have students draw a picture of their favorite season. Encourage them to label their pictures with the name of the season or with other words describing their pictures.

- Ask students to take a sheet of drawing paper and fold it in half once in one direction and then once in the other direction so when it is unfolded the paper is divided into four sections. Write the words *spring, summer, autumn,* and *winter* on the chalkboard. Ask students to draw a picture in the first section that shows what they like about spring, draw a picture in the second section that shows what they like about summer, and so on. Encourage students to think of special events or activities that happen during each of these seasons. Have students write the name of each season in the appropriate section and add captions below each picture to describe what they drew. Ask students to then share their pictures with the class.

I found them!

But look, Mom, now my boots are too small.

56

Time to Write!

Have you ever lost something?
Draw a picture.
Write about your picture.

57

Making Connections

Activity Links

- Explore the four seasons by having students think of ways that weather and plants change throughout the year. Make a class chart of the changes that occur during each season.
- Have students dress up in the clothing they wear during their favorite season, or have them make clothing for paper dolls or puppets for each season.
- Tell students to think about a place to hide something in the classroom. Have them give verbal clues. Then have other children guess where the items could be hidden.

Reading Links

You might want to include these books in a discussion of seasons:
- *Season to Season* by Christine Price (Steck-Vaughn Company, 1997).
- *The Snowy Day* by Ezra Jack Keats (Puffin Books, 1962).
- *That's What Happens When It's Spring* by Elaine Good (Good Books, 1987).

Writing

Ask students to follow along at the top of page 57 as you read the directions aloud. Have them draw a picture showing what they did when they lost something. Encourage students to write about their picture at the bottom of the page.

Walk around the room and encourage students as they are drawing. This is a good opportunity for you to work individually with students to learn how many are able to connect the story to personal experiences by drawing pictures. You can learn more about their ideas if you occasionally ask them to explain their drawings or if you write a dictated response for them.

Sharing

When students have finished their drawings, organize students into pairs. Ask them to describe the personal experiences illustrated in their drawings to their partners.

The Tests

The next three selections are similar to standardized-test reading comprehension passages, with questions at the end of each selection. You will be working with students as they progress through the three test sections, which can be administered in different sittings. You can use this test section to provide more practice thinking along by pausing occasionally as you read aloud to ask your students: "What are you thinking about now?" Giving your students this opportunity can help them realize that thinking along can make them better test-takers.

Note that these selections are not designed to test specific reading strategies, but rather are designed to show students how thinking along will help them comprehend and better answer questions about stories.

Introducing the Tests to Students

Tell students that you are going to read more stories aloud and they will answer questions about each story after you have finished reading. Point out that thinking about the story as it is read will make answering questions at the end of the story easier.

Thinking Along on Tests

Read the stories.
Answer the questions.

Where will the robin live?

The robin sees a fat worm.
Hop … hop … hop … hop.

"The robin needs a place to live,"
the girl says.
"After I eat," the robin says.
Hop … hop … hop … hop.

The girl has a house for the robin.
"Here is your house, Robin," she says.
But the robin doesn't come to it.
Hop … hop … hop … hop.

58

Say: *Open your books to page 58.*

Check to be sure all students are on the correct page.

Say: *This story is called "Where will the robin live?" Think about that question as we read the story.*

Say: *I will read the story about the robin while you follow along. Then I will read it a second time while you follow along again.
Now listen carefully as I read this story about the robin.*

Follow along in your book.

Read the story about the robin aloud. Remember to pause and ask the students to tell what they are thinking—to think along—with the story as you are reading. Next, read the story a second time.

A little bird goes flying by.
"Oh, hurry, Robin!" the girl says.
"Another bird will get your house."
The robin does not seem to care.
Hop … hop … hop … hop.

"I have to eat first," Robin says.
"Thank you just the same.
Let the little bird have the house.
I will build my nest in a tree.
That would be the best for me."
Hop … hop … hop … hop.

Sample: Where is the robin?

○
in the house

○
in the nest

○
on the ground

59

Each of the test sections is followed by four multiple-choice questions and one open-ended question. The question format is typical of many standardized and criterion-referenced tests. The purpose-setting question format at the beginning of each selection is similar to that used on many nationally standardized tests.

Say: *Look at the bottom of the page and find the question that says "Sample."*

Write *Sample* on the chalk-board.

Say: *Put your finger on the sample question and look at the three pictures under the question. Listen carefully as I read you the sample question.*

Sample Question: *"Where is the robin?"*
• *Is it in the house?*
• *Is it in the nest?*
• *Is it on the ground?*
Now use your pencil to fill in the circle under the picture that shows where the robin is in the story.

Demonstrate on the chalk-board how the correct answer should be marked. Pause while students mark their answers. Then call on a volunteer to answer the question.

Say: *That's right. In the story the robin is always hopping on the ground. You will fill in the circle under the picture that shows the ground.*

Check to be sure all students have marked the correct answer. If any have marked the wrong picture, allow them to erase that circle and fill in the correct circle.

Say: *Even if there were no words with this story, you can tell what the right answer is by looking at the pictures. Pictures can give good clues about the main idea in a story.*

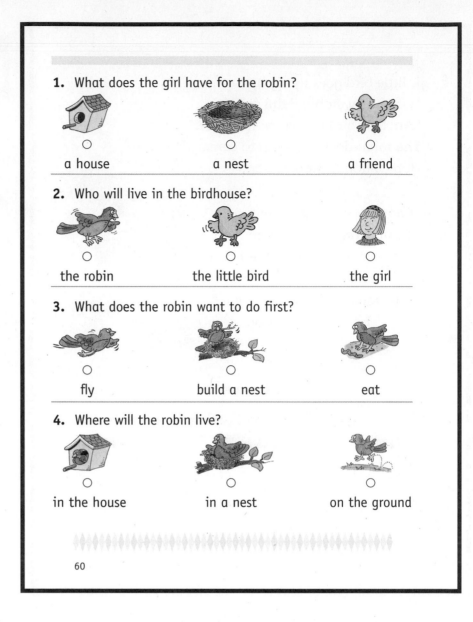

1. What does the girl have for the robin?

    ○ a house   ○ a nest   ○ a friend

2. Who will live in the birdhouse?

    ○ the robin   ○ the little bird   ○ the girl

3. What does the robin want to do first?

    ○ fly   ○ build a nest   ○ eat

4. Where will the robin live?

    ○ in the house   ○ in a nest   ○ on the ground

60

Say: *Now you will answer the rest of the questions. Find question 1 on this page. Put your finger on question number 1 and listen as I read it.*

Check to see that all students have found question 1.

Say: *Listen carefully as I read you question number 1.*

Question 1: *"What does the girl have for the robin?"*
- *Is it a house?*
- *Is it a nest?*
- *Is it a friend?*

Find the picture that shows what the girl has for the robin. Use your pencil to fill in the circle under the correct picture. Remember, if you change your mind, you can erase your answer and fill in the circle under another picture.

Pause while students mark their answers.

Use these steps to assist students in reading and answering questions 2–4.

5. What does the robin do all through the story?
   Draw a picture. Write about your picture.

Say: *Now you will draw a picture in the box. The picture will be about a question. Listen carefully and follow along as I read the question.*
Question 5: *"What does the robin do all through the story?"*
Draw a picture that shows what the robin is doing in this story. Try to write some words that tell about your picture on the line at the bottom of the page.

Answers and Analysis

1. a house; literal
2. the little bird; inferential
3. eat; literal
4. in a nest; literal
5. Evaluative/critical.

Students' drawings should show the robin hopping, eating a worm, or doing something else that is supported by the story. Student captions should not be scored but can provide good material for discussion.

Scoring Question 5:
2 = A good drawing will show the robin doing an activity that is supported by the story.
0 = A weak drawing will not show the robin, or will not show the robin doing activities supported by the story.

Explanation of Comprehension Skills

Literal: The answer is specifically stated in the text.
Inferential: The answer can be inferred from the text, but it is not specifically stated.
Evaluative/Critical: The answer is based on an evaluation of the text.

What happened to the castle?

Tillie and Willie went down to the sea.

They saw Sarah sitting in the sand.

Her dog Dingo barked at them.

Let's make a castle!" Sarah said.

Willie played in the waves.

"Let's all swim!" he cried.

"Come up here, Willie," Tillie called.

"Come and help us with the castle."

They all made a castle.

It was big and beautiful.

But the waves washed up close to it.

"The waves have followed Willie,"

Sarah said.

Say: *We are going to read another story together. This story is called "What happened to the castle?" We will read this story the same way we read the last one. First I will read the story aloud while you follow along, and then I will read it a second time. When we have finished reading, you will answer some questions about the story.*

Look at the top of the page. Now listen carefully as I read this story about the castle. Follow along in your book. Put your finger on the place where the story begins.

Read the story about the castle aloud. Remember to pause and ask students to tell what they are thinking—to think along—with the story as you are reading. Next, read the story a second time.

Soon the waves washed away the castle.
Dingo hid his head.
"How sad!" Sarah cried.
"Oh, no," Tillie said.
"Tomorrow we'll make a new one!"

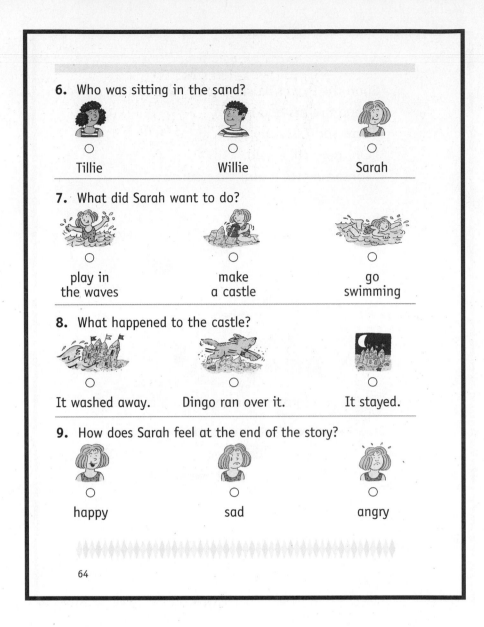

6. Who was sitting in the sand?

○ Tillie   ○ Willie   ○ Sarah

7. What did Sarah want to do?

○ play in the waves   ○ make a castle   ○ go swimming

8. What happened to the castle?

○ It washed away.   ○ Dingo ran over it.   ○ It stayed.

9. How does Sarah feel at the end of the story?

○ happy   ○ sad   ○ angry

64

Say: *Now you are going to answer questions about this story. I will read the questions aloud, and you will fill in the circle under the picture that best answers each question.*

Read questions 6–9 one at a time, turning the options under the pictures into questions, such as the following:

Question 6: *"Who was sitting in the sand?"*
- *Was it Tillie?*
- *Was it Willie?*
- *Was it Sarah?*
Find the picture and the word that tell who was sitting in the sand. Use your pencil to fill in the circle under the correct picture. Remember, if you change your mind, you can erase your answer and fill in the circle under another picture.

Walk around the room as you read to verify that students understand how to fill in the appropriate circles. Use these steps to assist students in reading and answering the remaining questions. Pause after reading each question and the answer choices to give students time to fill in each circle.

10. What did the children make?
Draw a picture. Write about your picture.

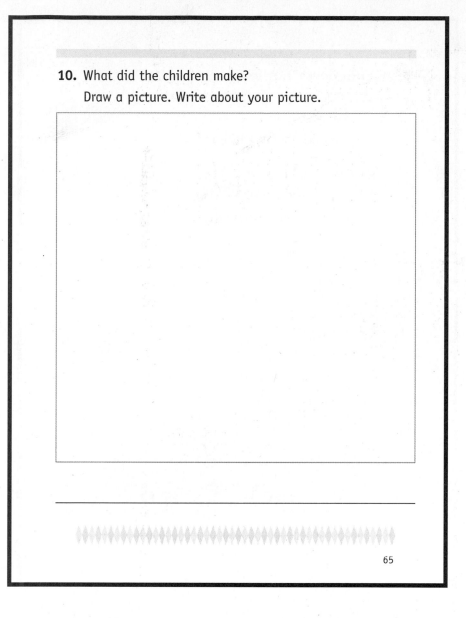

Say: *Now you will draw a picture in the box. The picture will be about a question. Listen carefully and follow along as I read the question.*

Question 10: *"What did the children make?"*
Draw a picture that shows what the children in the story made. Try to write some words that tell about your picture on the line at the bottom of the page.

Answers and Analysis

6. Sarah; literal
7. make a castle; inferential
8. It washed away. literal
9. sad; evaluative/critical
10. Evaluative/critical.

A correct drawing should show a sand castle. Student captions should not be scored but can provide good material for discussion.

Scoring Question 10:

2 = A good drawing will show a sand castle, and anything else that was mentioned in the story.

0 = A weak drawing will not show a sand castle.

Explanation of Comprehension Skills

Literal: The answer is specifically stated in the text.
Inferential: The answer can be inferred from the text, but it is not specifically stated.
Evaluative/Critical: The answer is based on an evaluation of the text.

What does Charlie do?
My cat Charlie
  is very, very old.
He's the oldest cat you'll see.

My cat Charlie
  is very, very orange.
He's orange as orange can be.

My cat Charlie
  sleeps all day long.
That's just what old cats do.

My cat Charlie
  goes out at night.
But he sleeps when he's out there, too.

Say: *We are going to read one more story together. This story is called "What does Charlie do?" We will read this story the same way we read the others. First I will read the story aloud while you follow along, and then I will read it a second time. When we have finished reading, you will answer some questions about the story.*

Look at the top of the page. Now listen carefully as I read this story about Charlie. Follow along in your book. Put your finger on the place where the story begins.

Read the story about Charlie aloud. Remember to pause and ask the students to tell what they are thinking—to think along—with the story as you are reading. Next, read the story a second time.

My cat Charlie
　　has yellow eyes.
At least I think he does.
He used to be a lively cat.
Well, maybe Charlie was.

My cat Charlie
　　is very, very old.
He doesn't fight or play.

My cat Charlie
　　is very, very orange.
And he sleeps both night and day.

67

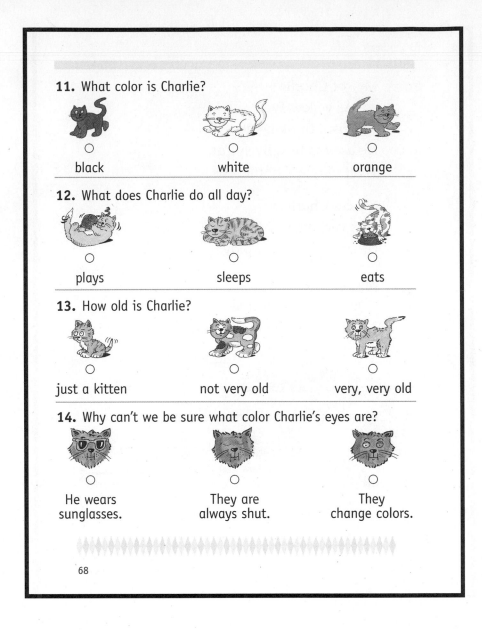

11. What color is Charlie?

○ black   ○ white   ○ orange

12. What does Charlie do all day?

○ plays   ○ sleeps   ○ eats

13. How old is Charlie?

○ just a kitten   ○ not very old   ○ very, very old

14. Why can't we be sure what color Charlie's eyes are?

○ He wears sunglasses.   ○ They are always shut.   ○ They change colors.

68

Say: *Now you are going to answer questions about this story. I will read the questions aloud, and you will fill in the circles under the picture that best answers each question.*

Read questions 11–14 one at a time, turning the options under the pictures into questions, such as the following:

Question 11: *"What color is Charlie?"*
• *Is he black?*
• *Is he white?*
• *Is he orange?*
Find the picture and the word that tell what color Charlie is. Use your pencil to fill in the circle under the correct picture. Remember, if you change your mind you can erase your answer and fill in the circle under another picture.

Walk around the room as you read to verify that students understand how to fill in the appropriate circles. Use these steps to assist students in reading and answering the remaining questions. Pause after reading each question and the answer choices to give students time to fill in each circle.

15. What does Charlie do outdoors at night?

Draw a picture. Write about your picture.

69

Making Connections

Discussion

After students have completed all three tests and you have graded them, give them back to students and review the questions and the correct answers. Read each story aloud once and then read each question, letting volunteers give the correct answers. Have students share their drawings with the class.

Scoring

Refer to the discussion of test taking on page T11 of the teacher's edition for information on scoring and interpreting student scores.

Say: *Now you will draw a picture in the box. The picture will be about a question. Listen carefully and follow along as I read the question.*

Question 15: *"What does Charlie do outdoors at night?" Draw a picture that shows what Charlie does outdoors at night. Try to write some words that tell about your picture on the line at the bottom of the page.*

Answers and Analysis

11. orange; literal
12. sleeps; literal
13. very, very old; literal
14. They are always shut. inferential
15. Evaluative/critical.

A correct drawing should show Charlie sleeping. Student captions should not be scored but can provide good material for discussion.

Scoring Question 15:

2 = A good drawing will show Charlie sleeping.

0 = A weak drawing will show Charlie doing something else besides sleeping, or will not show Charlie.

Explanation of Comprehension Skills

Literal: The answer is specifically stated in the text.

Inferential: The answer can be inferred from the text, but it is not specifically stated.

Evaluative/Critical: The answer is based on an evaluation of the text.

Thinking About...

The Main Idea of the Story

Identifying the Main Idea

Identifying the main idea in a story is critical for reading comprehension. By identifying the main idea, readers can separate details from major themes. This will help keep them from getting distracted by less important ideas in the story. The activities in this unit will help students apply the strategy of identifying the main idea. This strategy will help them to better understand and remember what they read.

Thinking About

The Main Idea of the Story

Read the story below.
Think about the main idea of the story.

Annie loves her cat, Tabby.
Every morning she feeds her.
Annie eats breakfast.
Tabby eats, too.
Annie goes to school.
Tabby can not go to school.
Tabby waits for Annie at home.
After school, Tabby and Annie play.
At night, Tabby sleeps on Annie's bed.
"Good night, Tabby," Annie says.
"Meow," Tabby says.

70

Introducing the Strategy

Ask for student volunteers to describe stories that they have heard or read. Then have them tell the class what the story was mainly about. Encourage them to describe the story's main idea in as few words as possible, rather than focusing on the details. To help direct students, ask questions such as the following:
- *Who was the story about?*
- *What happened in the story?*
- *How did the story end?*

Applying the Strategy

Ask students to follow along as you read the story in the pupil book. Tell them to think about the main idea in the story as you are reading.

What is this story mainly about?
Draw a picture.

This story made me think that pets are fun!

Write about your picture.

_____

Read and Think

- Read the stories.
- Stop at each box. Answer the question.
- Think about the main idea.

71

Read and Think

- Tell students that answering the questions in the boxes and drawing pictures will help them think about the stories.
- Encourage them to think about the most important part of each story.
- Ask them to write words or sentences below their pictures that tell the main idea of the story.

Presenting the Stories

Many beginning readers may have difficulty reading independently. As students read the stories, walk around the room to make sure that they are understanding the sentences. Ask them questions to facilitate understanding of any words giving them difficulty. Then encourage them to reread any sentences that they initially had trouble reading. As students are reading, they will be asked to write responses in question boxes that appear throughout the pupil's edition text. The teacher's edition provides possible student responses and teacher tips that focus on the strategy of identifying the main idea.

Discussing the Strategy

Have students draw a response to the question on page 71. Encourage students to include written responses with their drawings. Ask students to share their responses with the class. Write their suggestions on the chalkboard, and have students agree on one main idea for the story.

Explain to students that they will use this strategy as they read the selections in this unit.

Soccer Game!

Strategy Focus

Identifying the main idea of a story.

Story at a Glance

This story describes a game of soccer.

Vocabulary

You may want to introduce these key words to your students:

goalie	*pass*
dribble	*goal*

Getting Students Started

• Introducing the Selection

Ask students to tell about the different games or sports they have played. Encourage students to describe the main idea and rules of each game or sport. Discuss the meanings of *goalie* and *goal*. Having students think about games and sports they have played will help them think about the main idea in "Soccer Game."

• Purpose for Reading

Students read to find out how to play soccer and which team wins the game.

Soccer Game!

By Grace Maccarone

 This story is about playing soccer. The blue team tells the story. Read the story to find out how to play soccer and who wins the game.

We start the game.
We're ready.
We aim.
We pass.

72

We fall.

They get the ball.

Away they go!

We're doomed!

Oh, no!

 1 What do the kids think will happen next?
Draw a picture. Write about it.

Strategy Tip

Tell students that thinking about the main idea in a story is like retelling in pictures or words the most important things that happened in the story.

Possible Responses
Question 1

They are going to score.
The student is making a prediction based on the reading. Ask, "Why do you think they are going to score?" or say, "Tell me about your picture."

A goal.
This response could use elaboration. Encourage the student to clarify his or her reponse by asking, "Who do you think is going to score a goal? What makes you think so?"

From this response, it is unclear whether this student is comprehending the selection. Ask the student to tell you about his or her picture. Ask, "What just happened in the story? What do you think will happen next in the story?"

It's in the air.
Our goalie is there!

2 What is the goalie's job?
Draw a picture. Write about it.

74

My brother guards the goal.
The student has written a response without including a picture, which should not be discouraged. He or she is demonstrating comprehension of the reading by connecting it to personal experience.

Stopping the ball.
This response shows comprehension of the story. Ask this student to share his or her drawing with the class and tell how it shows what the goalie's job is.

Some students may not be ready to write their own captions. Ask this student to tell you about his or her picture.

We dribble.
We pass.
We slip on the grass.

We kick. We run.
We're having fun!

ESOL

Make cards that each have one rhyming word written on it from the story: *game* and *aim*; *fall* and *ball*; *air* and *there*; *pass* and *grass*; *hole* and *goal*; and *in* and *win*. Ask students to match the pairs of rhyming words. Then organize students into pairs and have them play a game of concentration using the rhyming word cards.

We see a hole.
We run to the goal.

77

After Reading

It is very important to have students read and discuss what they have drawn and written in the boxes.

Discussing the Think-Alongs

- Give as many students as possible a chance to share what they have drawn and written in one of the boxes.
- Have students explain what they were thinking when they drew and wrote their responses.
- Ask students how thinking about the main idea in a story helps them better understand and enjoy what they are reading.

Reteaching

For those students who have not drawn or are having difficulty with the activity:

- Read the story aloud while they read along with you, taking breaks to ask them to tell what they are think-ing as you are reading aloud.
- Have students work with a partner to read the story and draw responses.
- Ask questions that moti-vate students to think about main idea in the story, such as the following:
  - *What do you think this story was mostly about?*
  - *Which part of the story did you like best?*
  - *Have you ever played soccer? What did you like best about it?*

The ball goes in.
Hooray! We win!

 3 What was the most important part of this story?
Draw a picture. Write about it.

78

Possible Responses Question 3

This response is unclear without an accompanying written response that can explain the drawing. Encourage the student to clarify his or her response by saying, "Tell me about your picture. Why did you decide to draw what you did?"

They won!
This response shows good comprehension of one of the important story ideas. Ask, "Why did you think this was the most important part of the story? What other parts of the story are important?"

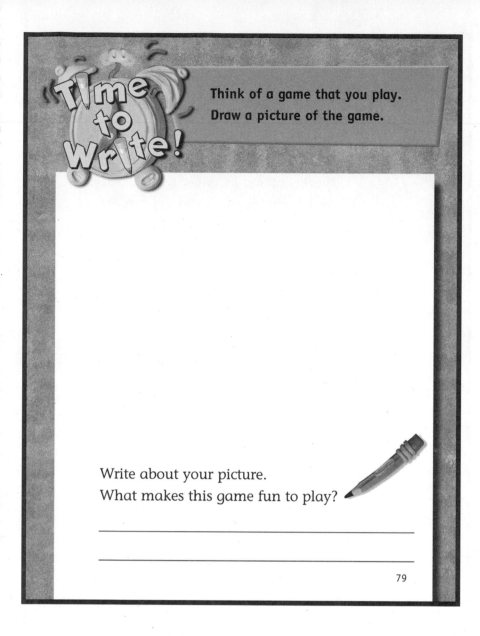

Time to Write!

Think of a game that you play.
Draw a picture of the game.

Write about your picture.
What makes this game fun to play?

_____

_____

79

Making Connections

Activity Links

- Ask students to give "show and tell" presentations to the class about their favorite sport or game.
- Have students read and discuss stories about famous athletes.
- Hold an "all sports day" at school during which students spend some time playing their favorite sport or game. Ask students to write about the sports day and what they liked best about it.
- To introduce sequencing, have students make a list of rules or directions for a game or activity. Then, make sentence strips of the different steps. Have students put the sentence strips into sequential order.

Reading Links

You may want to include the following books in a discussion of sports and athletic activities:
- _The Little Ballerina_ by Katharine Ross (Random House, 1996).
- _I Know Karate_ by Mary Packard (Scholastic, 1995).
- _How to Play the All-Star Way_ by Paul Joseph (Abdo, 1996).

They are having fun.

This response shows a good understanding of one of the important story ideas. "Why do you think this was the most important part of the story?"

Writing

Have students read the instructions for the drawing and writing activity. While students are completing their responses, walk around the room and encourage them as they draw. You can learn more about their thinking if you occasionally ask them to explain their drawings.

Sharing

Have students share their pictures with the class and talk about why they drew what they did.

Strategy Focus

Identifying the main idea of a story.

Story at a Glance

Yin-May gets the chicken pox and cannot go to her friend Emma's birthday party. But Emma finds a clever way to bring the party to Yin-May.

Vocabulary

You may want to introduce the following words to your students:

surprise   spots
string   letter
basket

Getting Students Started

• Introducing the Selection

Introduce the story by telling students that they are going to read about a girl named Yin-May who cannot go to her friend's birthday party because she is sick. Ask students to think about times they have not been able to go someplace they wanted to go because they were sick. Ask, "Where weren't you able to go?" "What did you do instead?"

• Purpose for Reading

Students read to find out how Yin-May gets to enjoy the party, too.

The Surprise Party

By Mary Cockett

 This story is about a girl named Yin-May. Yin-May cannot go to her friend's party. Read to find out how Yin-May gets to enjoy the party, too.

Yin-May had spots.
She had spots on her face and spots
on her neck and spots on her arms.
She had to stay in bed.

1 Draw a picture of Yin-May.

80

Possible Responses
Question 1

ths hr
At early grades, there will be some responses with scribbled wording or invented spelling like this one, which may be difficult to decipher.

However, the important thing is that students are thinking about the story and getting their ideas down on the page. Have this student tell about what he or she has written. Say, "What did you write here?" and "Tell me about your picture."

She's sick like me.
This response demonstrates comprehension of the main idea of the story so far, and also shows the student making a personal connection with the story character.

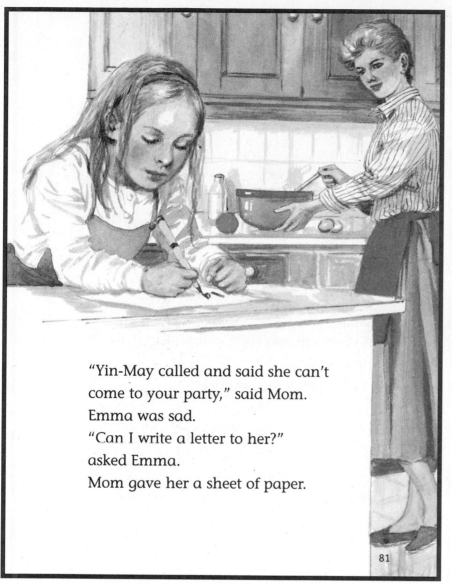

"Yin-May called and said she can't come to your party," said Mom.
Emma was sad.
"Can I write a letter to her?" asked Emma.
Mom gave her a sheet of paper.

81

Strategy Tip

Tell students that retelling the important parts of the story with pictures will help them think about the main idea in the story they are reading.

Encourage this student to tell more about his or her drawing. Say, "Tell me about your picture." Then, ask the student to retell what has happened so far in the story.

Emma wrote a letter to Yin-May.
This is what Emma wrote.

I am sorry you can't come
to my party.
Look out of your window
today at six o'clock.
Have a long piece of string
in your hand.
Love,
Emma

to
Yin-
May

82

Reinforcing the Strategies

Ask
students to
recall a time in their lives when
they could not do something
that they wanted to do. Ask
them to tell why they could not
do what they wanted to do and
what they did instead.

Yin-May read the letter.
"Emma is my best friend," she said.
"I wonder what the string is for."
"I don't know," said Yin-May's mom.
She found a very long piece of string
for Yin-May.

83

At six o'clock Yin-May
looked out of her window.
"What a surprise," she said.
She saw all her friends
who had been at Emma's party.
They had balloons and party hats.
They clapped their hands and waved
when they saw Yin-May at the window.

2 Draw a picture of Yin-May's friends.

84

Possible Responses
Question 2

Her friends are outside the house. They are playing.
Some students may be ready to write responses without pictures at this point. Do not discourage this. Think about your students' abilities when determining how it would be best to encourage them to respond to the questions. Ask this student, "Why are her friends outside the house?"

They are in the yard.
This response shows an understanding of the main event in the story, and also shows an understanding of details by the inclusion of the party hats and balloons in the picture.

If students do not label their pictures, it will be useful to have them talk about their pictures. Ask, "Tell me about your picture. Why did you decide to draw what you did?"

"Let down the string, Yin-May,"
said Emma.
"But keep one end in your hand."
So Yin-May let down the string and
Emma tied the end to a basket.
Then all her friends put a present
for Yin-May in the basket.

"The Surprise Party" provides a good opportunity for students to share their birthday customs with the rest of the class. Have students from other countries talk about traditional birthday celebrations in their home countries. Have students from the United States talk about special family birthday traditions.

85

After Reading

It is very important to have students read and discuss what they have drawn and written in the boxes.

Discussing the Think-Alongs

- Give as many students as possible a chance to share what they have drawn or written in one of the boxes.
- Have students explain what they were thinking when they drew and wrote their responses.
- Ask students to tell in their own words the story of "The Surprise Party."

Reteaching

For students who have not drawn or are having difficulty with the activity:

- Read the story aloud while they read along with you, taking breaks to ask them to tell what they are thinking as you are reading aloud.
- Ask questions that motivate students to think about the main idea in the story. Have students look at the pictures carefully to aid comprehension. Ask students to tell the story by looking at the pictures.
- Have students work with a partner to read the story and draw responses.

There were balloons and candy and cards and a big piece of birthday cake from Emma.
"You are a good friend," said Yin-May.
"Now I can join in the party, too."

 3 Draw a picture of Yin-May at the end of the story.

86

Possible Responses
Question 3

She got to go to the party.
This response shows comprehension of the story by retelling the story with a picture. You may want to have this student share his or her picture with the class and tell about how he or she thinks that Yin-May got to go to the party.

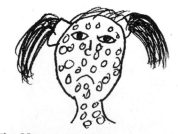

Yin-May
It is not clear from this picture and label that this student understands what happened at the end of the story. Ask this student to describe what he or she wrote and drew: "Tell me about your picture. How do you think Yin-May felt at the beginning of the story? How has this changed at the end of the story?"

Think of a party you went to. Draw a picture of you and your friends at a party.

Write about your picture.
Where was the party?

_____

_____

87

Making Connections

Activity Links

- Help each student put together a "birthday basket" for someone with whom he or she is close.
- Have students write a song (to the tune of a song they know) that the other children might have sung to Yin-May when they gave her the basket of presents.
- Create a classroom get-well card for someone who is sick.
- Have students act out the story. Have student volunteers be Yin-May, Yin-May's mother, Emma, and Emma's mother. The rest of the students can be friends at Emma's birthday party.

Reading Links

You may want to include the following books in a discussion of birthdays:

- *Arthur's Birthday* by Marc Tolon Brown (Little Brown & Co., 1991).
- *A Birthday Basket for Tia* by Pat Mora (Aladdin Paperbacks, 1990).
- *Birthdays!: Celebrating Life Around the World* by Eve B. Feldman (Bridgewater Books, 1996).

She's happy.
This student is showing how Yin-May felt at the end of the story. Ask, "Why do you think Yin-May was happy at the end of the story?"

Writing

Have students read the instructions for the drawing and writing activity. While the students are drawing pictures of themselves at a party, walk around the room and encourage students in their drawing and writing. You can learn more about their thinking if you occasionally ask them to explain their drawings.

Sharing

When students have finished, have them share their responses with the rest of the class and tell about what they drew and wrote.

Pet Day

Strategy Focus

Identifying the main idea of a story.

Story at a Glance

The girl in the story searches for a special pet to take to class on Pet Day.

Vocabulary

You may want to introduce the following words to your students:
pet
prize
shyest
trained
funniest

Getting Students Started

- **Introducing the Selection**

Ask students to think about the different pets that people might have. Ask questions such as the following:
- *How do people decide what pets they might want to have?*
- *Why do some animals not make good house pets?*

Call on students to share their ideas about pets.

- **Purpose for Reading**

Students read to find out what pet the girl will bring to Pet Day.

Pet Day

By Lois Bick

Let's Read

This story is about Pet Day. Read the story to find out what pets the students bring to school on Pet Day.

On Pet Day, all the kids take their pets to school. Every pet wins a prize.

1 What pet would you like to bring? Draw a picture. Write about it.

88

Possible Responses
Question 1

Tabby
Students at this stage may write very brief captions for their pictures. These responses show that the students are comprehending and understanding what Pet Day is.

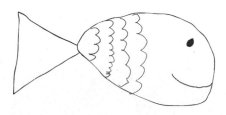

fish
To encourage students to elaborate on their responses, you can ask them to read their captions and ask them questions about their pictures and captions, such as: "Is Tabby your cat?" "Is that your pet fish?" and "What color is your fish?"

Last year on Pet Day,
Jerome's dog won a prize.
The dog is very big.

Marcy's snake won a prize.
The snake is very long.

89

Strategy Tip

Tell students that thinking about the main idea in the story as they read will be like retelling in pictures or words the most important things that happened in the story.

my dog

This student shows an understanding of the story by relating it to personal experience. Ask, "What kind of dog do you have? Would your dog like to visit the class during Pet Day?"

Juan's bird won a prize.
The bird is very loud.
Cassie's rabbit won
a prize, too.
The rabbit has pretty eyes.
But I didn't win anything
because I don't have a pet.

2 How does the girl telling the story feel?
Draw a picture. Write about it.

Possible Responses
Question 2

Left out

This student shows that he or she empathizes with the character and understands the main idea of this section of the story. Ask, "Why do you think the girl would feel left out if she does not have a pet?"

If students do not write captions for their pictures, encourage them to talk about their pictures. Ask this student, "How is the girl in your picture feeling? Why does she feel that way?"

She has pet.

Some students may be ready to write responses without drawing pictures. However, it is unclear from this response whether this student understands the question. Encourage the student to clarify what he or she was thinking by asking, "Does the girl have a pet? If the girl does not have a pet, how do you think she might feel?" If the student is still confused about the main idea of the story, read the story aloud to the student as he or she follows along.

This year I had an idea.
I went outside by the front steps,
and I started to hunt.

Then I found something special
to take to school.

I knew that my pets would win
a prize this year.

91

Meeting Individual Needs

Read the story aloud while students follow along. Stop as you read so that students can copy or write the name of each character in the story. Next to each character's name, have students write or draw the animal that this character is bringing to Pet Day.

Jerome brought his mouse.
He chased it most of the day.
Marcy carried her guinea pig.
She let everyone hold it.

92

Juan held his turtle.
He couldn't get it to
come out of its shell.

Cassie walked in with her monkey.
She trained it to do tricks.

93

After Reading

It is very important to have students read and discuss what they have drawn and written in the boxes.

Discussing the Think-Alongs

- Give as many students as possible a chance to share what they have drawn and written in one of the boxes.
- Have students explain what they were thinking when they drew and wrote.
- Ask students to tell in their own words what the story "Pet Day" is about.

Reteaching

For those students who have not drawn or are having difficulty with the activity:

- Have them read along with you while you read the story aloud. Take breaks to ask students to tell what they are thinking about as you are reading aloud.
- Have students work with a partner to read and discuss the story and draw responses.
- Ask questions that motivate students to think about main ideas in the story, such as the following:
  - *What is Pet Day?*
  - *If our class had Pet Day, what animal would you bring?*
  - *What did the girl in the story do so that she could bring a pet to Pet Day?*

And do you know what?
My pets won a prize, too.
And everyone loved catching
my grasshoppers.

 3 Draw a picture of the classroom on Pet Day. Write about Pet Day.

94

Possible Responses Question 3

Pets at school.

They bring pets.
These responses show comprehension of the story and an understanding of the main idea. Ask students to share their pictures with the class and talk about what they chose to draw.

Time to Write!

Think of a pet you have or a pet you would like to have.

Draw a picture of you and a pet.

Write about your picture.
What prize would your pet win on Pet Day?

_____

_____

95

When students do not write captions for their drawings, ask them to discuss their pictures. Ask this student, "What kind of insect did you draw? Do you have a pet insect?"

Writing

Have students read the instructions for the drawing and writing activity. While the students are completing their responses, walk around the room and encourage students with their pictures. You can learn more about their thinking if you ask them to explain their drawings.

Sharing

Make a list of students' choices for pets and prizes. From this information, have the class determine the most popular pet, the most unusual pet, and other prizes.

Making Connections

Activity Links

- Make a list on the chalkboard of the animals that students in the story brought to Pet Day. Then, make another list with the prizes that different pets won on Pet Day. Have the class match the pets with the different prizes.
- Tell a story about a pet you have had. Ask the students to listen to your story and then say what prize they think your pet should receive.
- Have students dictate stories to you about their own pets or pets they would like to have. Write the stories in folded booklets that the students can illustrate and share with the class.
- Take a field trip to a local zoo, farm, or petting zoo. Have students draw and write about their favorite animals, telling whether or not they would make a good pet.

Reading Links

You might want to include these books in a discussion of animals as pets:

- *Bedtime Cat* by Lynn Reiser (Greenwillow Books, 1991).
- *Digby* by Barbara Shook Hazen (Harper Trophy, 1997).
- *I Have a Pet* by Shari Halpern (Simon & Schuster Books, 1994).

What Might Happen Next

Making Predictions

Making predictions while reading makes reading more meaningful. By making predictions about what will happen next, readers can anticipate the events in a story. This will probably not be the first time your students have used this strategy. Young readers often make predictions when listening to repetitive stories. However, this activity will help your students realize how consciously thinking about making predictions makes reading easier and more interesting.

Thinking About

What Might Happen Next

Read the story below.
What do you think will happen?

> A caterpillar sat in the warm sun.
> A bee flew by.
> "You can fly," said the caterpillar.
> The caterpillar tried to fly, but he could not.
> He felt very sad.
> The caterpillar fell asleep.
> He slept for a long time.
> When he woke up, he was surprised.
> He had large wings with bright colors.
> He could fly!
> Now he was a butterfly.
> And he was happy.

96

Introducing the Strategy

Choose an unfamiliar, yet predictable story, such as *The True Story of the Three Little Pigs*, that you have not read to your students in class. Read the first page of the story and ask your students to think about what might happen next in the story. Ask students to generate as many predictions as possible before you read further in the story. You may need to give students some ideas at first.

Applying the Strategy

Ask students to follow along as you read the story in the pupil book, or have a volunteer read it. After each sentence, stop reading, or ask the student to stop reading, and ask the class what they think might happen next in the story.

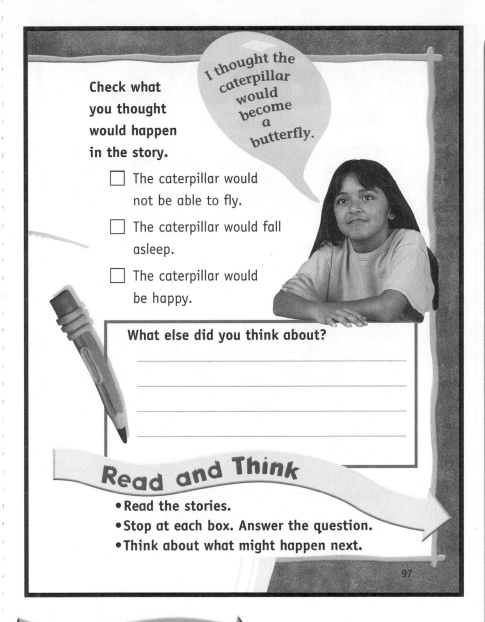

Check what
you thought
would happen
in the story.

I thought the caterpillar would become a butterfly.

☐ The caterpillar would
not be able to fly.

☐ The caterpillar would fall
asleep.

☐ The caterpillar would
be happy.

What else did you think about?

_____

_____

_____

_____

Read and Think

• Read the stories.
• Stop at each box. Answer the question.
• Think about what might happen next.

97

Read and Think

- Remind students that answering the questions in the boxes will help them think about the stories.
- Tell them that they can draw a picture beside their writing to help show what they are thinking.
- Encourage them to think about what might happen next in the stories as they read.

Presenting the Stories

Most students should be able to read the stories in this unit independently. As students read, walk around the room to make sure that they are understanding each sentence. Ask them questions to facilitate understanding of any words giving them difficulty. Then encourage them to reread any sentences that they initially had trouble reading. As students are reading, they will be asked to write responses in question boxes that appear throughout the pupil's edition text. The teacher's edition provides possible student responses and teacher tips that focus on the strategy of making predictions.

Discussing the Strategy

After finishing the story, read the answer choices aloud. Have students complete the activity independently or orally in small groups. Ask students questions such as the following:

- *What made you think the caterpillar would not be able to fly?*
- *What made you think the caterpillar would change?*
- *What made you think the caterpillar would be happy?*

Tell students that it is not important if what they think might happen next in a story does not happen. It is also not important if they did not think about all of the things in the list that follows the story. It is only important that they were thinking about what might happen next in the story. Explain to students that they will be thinking about what might happen next as they read the stories in the unit.

97

My Boat

My Boat

By Kay Davies and Wendy Oldfield

Strategy Focus

Making predictions about what will happen next in a story.

Story at a Glance

This story tells about different kinds of toy boats made from plastic, paper, clay, and wood.

Vocabulary

You may want to introduce these key words to your students:

floats *sail*
waves *keel*
mast

Getting Students Started

· Introducing the Selection

Ask students to think about different kinds of toy boats and real boats. Draw a simple picture of a sailboat on the chalkboard. Ask students to describe the different parts of a boat, such as the sail, and discuss how boats are able to move across the water. Have students share any experiences they have had with real boats or toy boats. Having students think about boats will help them make predictions as they read this selection.

· Purpose for Reading

Students read to think about what kind of boat they would like to have.

Let's Read

This story is about different boats. Read the story to find out what the different boats can do.

Look at all these boats!
How many can you see?
What colors and shapes are they?

98

98

My boat is long and red.
My boat is flat at one end
and pointed at the other end.

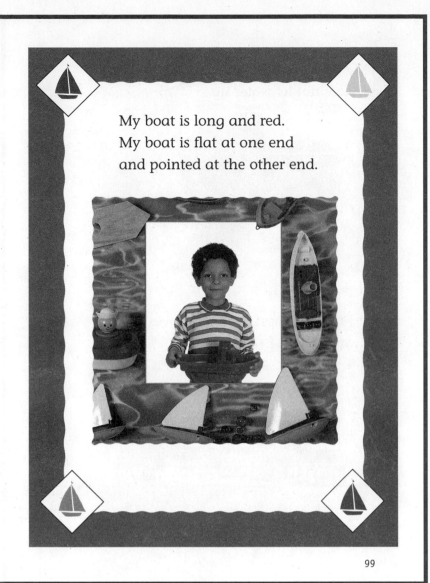

99

Strategy Tip
Tell students that thinking about what might happen next while they read is fun and will help them understand what they are reading.

My boat floats on water.
It does not let water in.

If I make waves, my boat moves
away from me.

100

Ask students acquiring English to write in the boxes in their first language if they can, and then tell you in English what they wrote.

What will happen if I put some marbles in my boat?

1 What do you think will happen if the boy puts marbles in the boat?

101

Possible Responses
Question 1

marbles heavy
Students may respond to the question with single related words in a kind of free association. In this case the student is thinking about what will happen when marbles are put into the boat. Ask, "What do you think will happen if heavy marbles are put into the boat?"

The boat might sink.
This response shows that the student is making a prediction based on a good understanding of the cause-and-effect relationship between adding marbles and the boat sinking.

I don't know.
Remind the student that there are no wrong answers to the question, and that it is fine to make a guess about what he or she thinks might happen. Encourage the student to respond by asking, "What do you think might happen if you put something heavy into a toy boat like this?"

If the marbles are all at one end of my boat —it sinks!

With marbles at both ends, my boat floats low in the water.

If I add too many marbles . . . !

 2 What do you think will happen if he adds more marbles?

Possible Responses
Question 2

It might tip over.

The boat sinks.

The marbles will fall out.

All three responses describe the possible effects of adding too many marbles to the boat, but each demonstrates a slightly different understanding of what will happen. The first and second responses suggest possible effects for the boat, and the third response focuses on what might happen to the marbles.

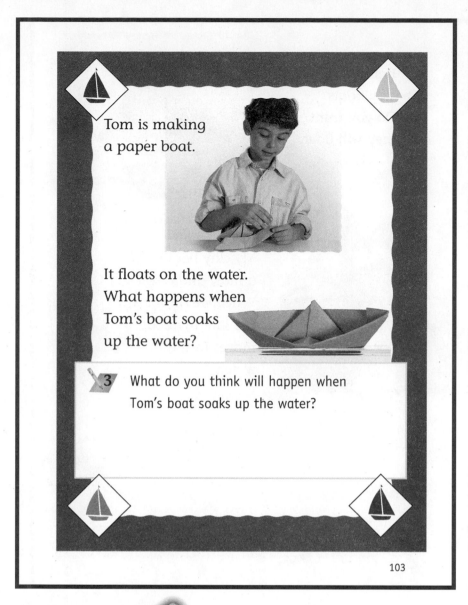

Tom is making a paper boat.

It floats on the water. What happens when Tom's boat soaks up the water?

3 What do you think will happen when Tom's boat soaks up the water?

103

Possible Responses
Question 3

The boat gets wet.
The student is predicting what will happen to the paper boat in the water. Encourage the student to continue predicting by asking, "Then what do you think will happen?"

It gets wet and then it sinks.
Students often use more than one strategy at a time. This student is not only predicting what will happen but is also showing an understanding of the cause-and-effect relationship between the boat getting wet and the boat sinking.

I don't want to be in that boat!
The student is making a personal connection, but is not directly addressing what will happen next. Ask, "Why wouldn't you want to be in that boat? What do you think will happen next?"

I'm making
clay boats.
Do you think
they will float?

My clay boat has
a mast and a sail.
When we blow on
the sail, my boat
moves in the
water.

 4   What else could you use to make a boat?

104

Possible Responses
Question 4

wood
> This response is brief, but
> the amount of writing is
> not important at this time.
> Nevertheless, encourage stu-
> dents to extend their
> responses. Ask, "Can you
> think of anything else you
> could use to make a boat?"

**A milk carton. I made one
like that.**
> The student is using back-
> ground information to
> respond to the story. Ask,
> "Did you use any other
> materials?"

I could paint a boat.
> The student is making a
> personal connection to the
> story and thinking about
> what he or she could do to
> make a boat.

I have made a wooden boat. With a drop of dishwashing liquid, my boat moves on its own.

105

Under Polly's wooden
boat, there is a keel.
It's hard to pull
Polly's boat over.
If I tip it sideways,
it swings back up again.

106

We are having a race with our boats.

107

Reinforcing the Strategies

Students can use other reading strategies to respond to the story. Have students practice retelling by drawing a picture of the most interesting thing they learned about boats. Also, have students share their own experiences with boats to relate the story to personal experience.

After Reading

It is very important to have the students read and discuss the predictions that they have made in the boxes.

Discussing the Think-Alongs

- Give as many students as possible a chance to tell what they wrote in one of the boxes.
- Have students explain what they were thinking when they wrote.
- Ask students how guessing what might happen next helps them think about the story.

Reteaching

For those students who have not written or are having difficulty with the activity:

- Ask students to tell what they were thinking about as they read.
- Model making predictions by sharing what you think will happen next as you read the story aloud.
- Ask questions that help students make predictions, such as the following:
  - *Have you ever sailed a toy boat? What happened?*
  - *How do boats move in the water?*
  - *How do they float?*

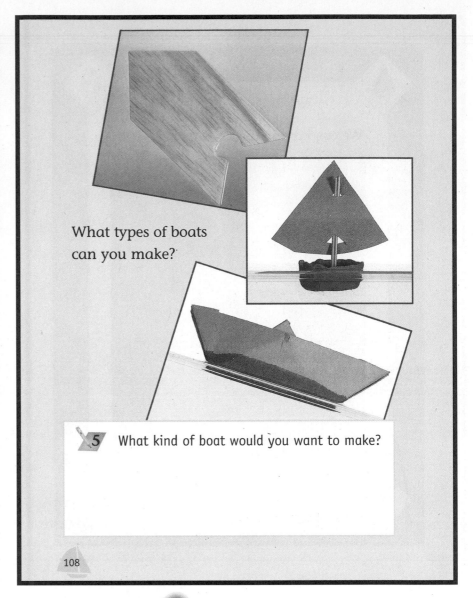

What types of boats can you make?

5 What kind of boat would you want to make?

108

Possible Responses
Question 5

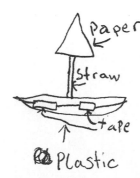

The student might be visualizing the kind of boat he or she could make, or demonstrating that he or she can make a boat by drawing one. Say, "Tell me more about your picture."

I might make a paper one.
The student is making a prediction. Ask, "What would your boat look like?"

I never made one.
The student is making a personal connection to the selection. Encourage the student to predict whether he or she could make a boat by thinking about the boats shown in this story. Ask, "Do you think you could make a boat like any of the ones in this story?

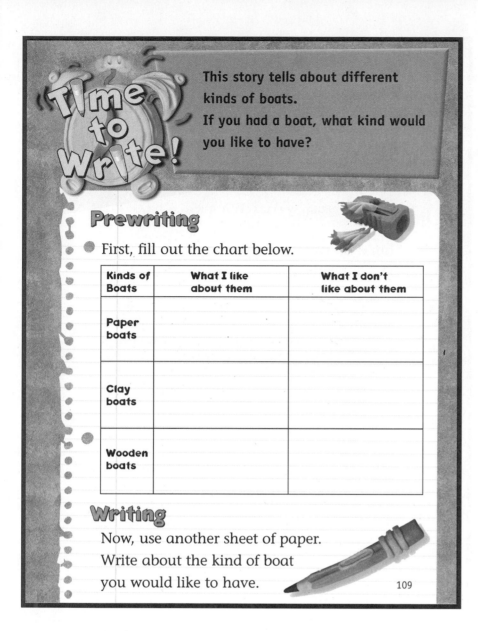

Time to Write!

This story tells about different kinds of boats.

If you had a boat, what kind would you like to have?

Prewriting

First, fill out the chart below.

Kinds of Boats	What I like about them	What I don't like about them
Paper boats		
Clay boats		
Wooden boats		

Writing

Now, use another sheet of paper.
Write about the kind of boat you would like to have.

109

Prewriting

Explain that the prewriting activity will help students think about what kind of boats they could have.

Writing

Remind students that they do not have to include everything from their prewriting responses—just the ideas that best help them tell what kind of boat they would like to have. Tell students that they can draw a picture of their boat as well to show what kind of boat they would like to have.

Sharing

When students have finished the writing activity, have volunteers read what they have written and have the class discuss where they would like to go with their boats.

Making Connections

Activity Links

- Have students make paper boats like the one shown in the story. There are many origami books available that will teach students to make boats and other paper objects.
- Ask students to work together in small groups to write and illustrate a story about a boy or girl who takes a ride in a boat. Encourage these groups to share their stories with the rest of the class.
- Have students try the experiment of putting a drop of soap in water to see if they can make a boat move. Have students explain what they think happened.

Reading Links

You might want to include the following books in a discussion about boats and experiments:
- *Amazing Boats* by Margaret Lincoln (Knopf, 1992).
- *50 Nifty Science Experiments* by Lisa Taylor Melton and Eric Ladizinsky (Contemporary Books, 1992).
- *My Visit to the Aquarium* by Aliki (HarperTrophy, 1996).

My New Boy

Strategy Focus

Making predictions about what will happen next in a story.

Story at a Glance

A little boy gets a new puppy, or a puppy gets a new boy.

Vocabulary

You may want to introduce the following words to your students:
tricks
lucky
smart

Getting Students Started

• *Introducing the Selection*

Introduce the story by asking your students to think about how it would feel to get a new pet. Ask your students to discuss any pets they have at home and what it was like to get the pets. Talk about what your students most like to do with their pets. Having students think about their own pets or pets they would like to have will help them think about the story they are going to read.

• *Purpose for Reading*

Tell students that they are going to read the story to find out about the things the puppy and boy do together.

My New Boy

By Joan Phillips

 This story is about a puppy who gets a new home with a little boy. Read the story to find out what the puppy does with his new boy.

I am a little black puppy.
I live in a pet store.

110

Soon I will have a kid of my own.
Many kids come.

 1 What do you think the kids will do with the puppy?

Strategy Tip

Tell students that thinking about what might happen next while they read is fun and will help them better understand what they are reading.

This one pulls my tail.

This one kisses too much.
They are not for me.

111

Possible Responses
Question 1

They will pet him.
This student makes a prediction, perhaps by drawing on personal experience.

pet
This response is appropriate, yet brief. Encourage students to write everything they are thinking about in the box. Say, "Can you think of anything else the kids might do? Draw a picture if it helps you think better."

pet feed run
Students may respond to the question with single related words in a kind of free association. This kind of response is appropriate because it helps students summarize what they have read. Encourage this student to write more ideas, or draw a picture to go with this response.

Here is another kid.

He says hello.

He pats my head.

Woof! Woof!

This is the boy for me!

My new boy takes me home.

I start taking care of my boy
right away.

 2 How do you think the puppy will take
care of the boy?

Possible Responses
Question 2

I don't know.

Encourage this student to
make a prediction by asking,
"What might the puppy and
boy do together? What are
some things that both the
puppy and the boy need?"

**The puppy will keep him
warm at night.**

In this response the student
is making a prediction based
on personal experience with
dogs or pets. Ask, "How will
the puppy keep the boy
warm?"

My dog makes me laugh.

Although this student is not
making a prediction, he or
she is relating personal experience to the story. Ask this
student, "Do you think the
puppy might make the boy
laugh?"

I help him eat dinner.

I keep him clean.

I teach him to play tug of war.

113

Ask students what it would be like to get new puppies of their own. If any students have puppies, encourage them to share their experiences. Have students suggest things that they might like to do with a puppy that aren't discussed in the story. Discuss with students how they would feel if they lost a pet, and how they would feel if they found a lost pet.

I teach him to throw a ball to me.
I show my boy tricks.
I sit up.
I roll over.
I teach my boy to give

me a bone every time I do a trick.
My boy is not good at everything.

 3 What do you think the puppy can do better than the boy?

114

Possible Responses
Question 3

Fetch the ball. My dog is good at fetch.

Students often use more than one strategy at a time. This student is not only making a prediction, but is also connecting personal experience to the story. Say, "What else might the puppy do better than the boy?"

I wonder what the puppy will do.

This student's response mirrors the question. To encourage this student to make a prediction, ask,

"What can a boy do? What can a puppy do? What do you think the puppy can do better than the boy?"

The puppy can dig for a bone.

In this response the student predicts what the puppy can do better than the boy. Ask, "How might the puppy dig for a bone? How might the boy dig for a bone?"

He can not dig very fast.

He can not scratch
his ears with his foot.

He can not hide under the bed.

115

My boy can not run as fast as I can.

I run and run.

Oh, no!

I do not see my boy.

Is he lost?

4 What do you think the puppy will do?

Possible Responses Question 4

go home

He will bark and look for his boy.

These students predict what the puppy might do.

Is he lost?

In this response the student questions the text, reflecting a close reading of the story. To encourage this student to make a prediction, ask, "Who do you think is lost? What do you think the puppy will do next?"

I look behind a tree.
I look on the rocks.
I do not see my boy.

117

Is he on the swing?
No.
Is he on the slide?
No.
I do not see my
boy anywhere.

Now I see my boy.
He sees me too.
He is happy I found him.

> **5** What do you think the puppy will say to
> the boy?

119

Possible Responses
Question 5

Do not lose me.
This student makes a valid pre-diction about what the puppy might say. Ask, "How do you think the puppy felt when he couldn't find the boy?"

I would be mad if my pup ran away.
This student did not answer the question, but was thinking about what he or she would do in the situation. Say, "That's great to think about what you would do. What do you think the puppy in this story might say to the boy?"

I am happy! The puppy is happy with the boy.
This student is not only predicting what the puppy might say to the boy but is also summarizing the puppy's feelings. Predicting and sum-marizing help students devel-op a broad overview of a text's meaning.

After Reading

It is very important to have the students read and discuss the predictions that they have written in the boxes.

Discussing the Think-Alongs

- Give as many students as possible a chance to tell what they wrote in one of the boxes.
- Have students explain what they were thinking when they wrote.
- Ask students how thinking about what might happen next helps them better understand and enjoy what they are reading.

Reteaching

For those students who have not written or are having difficulty with the activity:

- Ask them to tell what they were thinking about as they read.
- Model your own use of prediction by talking about what you think might happen next in the story as you read it aloud.
- Ask questions that motivate students to make predictions about what might happen next in the story, such as the following:
  - *What do you think the puppy and boy would like to do together?*
  - *Do you think the puppy will look for his boy?*
  - *How do you think the puppy will feel when he finds the boy?*

We go home.
Woof! Woof! Woof!
I tell my boy he must not get lost again.
My boy is lucky to have a smart puppy
like me!

120

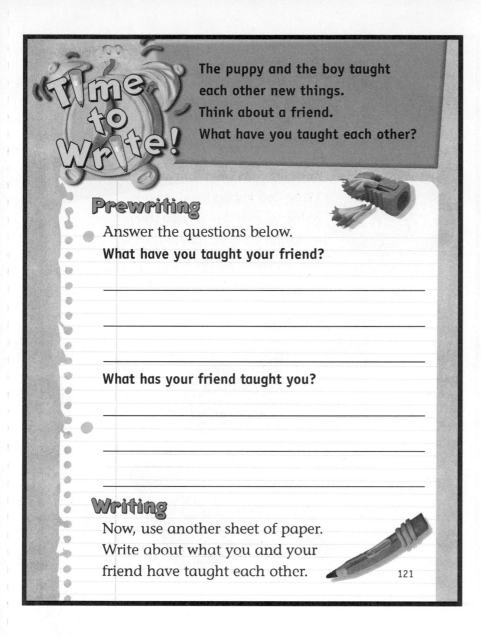

Time to Write!

The puppy and the boy taught each other new things. Think about a friend. What have you taught each other?

Prewriting

Answer the questions below.

What have you taught your friend?

_____

_____

_____

What has your friend taught you?

_____

_____

_____

Writing

Now, use another sheet of paper. Write about what you and your friend have taught each other.

121

Making Connections

Activity Links

- Have students draw a picture of their pets, or a pet they would like to have. Ask them to write captions that describe what they like to do with their pets.
- Read another story to the class and stop at different points to ask them to make predictions about what might happen next.
- Have students make a collage illustrating the different activities they can do with pets, or that features friends helping each other learn or having fun together.

Reading Links

You may want to introduce these books in a discussion about different kinds of friendships:

- *My Dinosaur* by Mark Alan Weatherby (Scholastic Trade, 1997).
- *Love You Forever* by Robert Munsch (Firefly Books, 1988).
- *The Giving Tree* by Shel Silverstein (HarperCollins, 1986).

Prewriting

Explain to students that the prewriting activity will help them think about what they have learned from a friend, and what they have helped a friend learn. Tell them that this will help them plan what they will write about. Students can work on the prewriting activity individually or in small groups.

Writing

Remind students that they do not have to include everything from their prewriting responses, just the ideas that help them best describe what they have learned from a friend and what they have helped their friend learn.

Sharing

When students have finished the writing activity, have volunteers read what they have written to the class. Help students make a bulletin board display of their writing about learning from friends.

Little Red and the Wolf
By Gare Thompson

Strategy Focus

Making predictions about what will happen next in a story.

Story at a Glance

Little Red Riding Hood gathers food for her grandmother and invites the Big Bad Wolf to dinner.

Vocabulary

You may want to introduce the following words to your students:

butcher	*tasty*
roast	*friendly*

Getting Students Started

- **Introducing the Selection**

  Ask students if they have ever heard the story of Little Red Riding Hood. Discuss what the story is about. Talk about Little Red Riding Hood, where she is going, and what happens to her. Encouraging students to think about the traditional version of this story will help them focus on the unique aspects of this selection.

- **Purpose for Reading**

  Students read to find out what happens to Little Red Riding Hood.

Let's Read

This story is about a little girl, Little Red Riding Hood, who is going to visit her grandmother. Read the story to find out who she meets along the way.

Once upon a time, Little Red Riding Hood went to visit Grandmother.

122

Strategy Tip

Tell students that thinking about what might happen next while they read is fun and will help them think about what they are reading.

Along the way, she passed the butcher. The butcher asked, "Where are you going, Little Red Riding Hood?" Little Red Riding Hood said, "I'm going to visit Grandmother." Then the butcher gave her a roast to take to Grandmother.

> **1** Who do you think will be watching Little Red Riding Hood?

123

Possible Responses Question 1

Big bad wolf.
This prediction reflects an appropriate use of background knowledge and shows good comprehension of the reading.

bear
This is an interesting response in which the student has substituted another animal for the traditional wolf, perhaps thinking of a different fairy tale. Ask, "Why do you think a bear might be following Little Red Riding Hood? What does the bear look like?"

Don't know.
Encourage students to respond to each question in writing or by drawing a picture. Ask this student to summarize what he or she learned from the class's discussion of the traditional Little Red Riding Hood tale, and then ask, "Who might be following Little Red Riding Hood in this story?"

Now Big Bad Wolf was hiding and watching.
Big Bad Wolf licked his lips and thought,
"Yum, yum. What a big roast she has.
I'm going to follow Little Red Riding Hood.
Maybe I'll get a tasty dinner."

2 Who do you think Little Red Riding Hood
will visit next?

124

Possible Responses
Question 2

Maybe her girl friend.
This is an appropriate, although
inaccurate, prediction. Ask,
"Do you think Little Red Riding
Hood might want to bring
more food to Grandmother for
dinner? Where else might she
go to get more food?"

a baker
This is an insightful prediction
that shows the student is
looking ahead in the story to
answer the questions and
make predictions. Ask, "Why
do you think she's going to
visit a baker next?"

her grandma
This is a good prediction based
on background knowledge of
the traditional tale. Ask, "Do
you think Little Red Riding
Hood might get more food
before she visits Grandmother?
What kinds of food would be
good with meat?"

Little Red Riding Hood walked on.
Along the way, she passed the baker.
The baker asked, "Where are you
going, Little Red Riding Hood?"
Little Red Riding Hood said, "I'm going
to visit Grandmother."
Then the baker gave her some warm
bread to take to Grandmother.

125

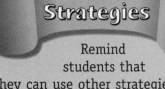

Remind
students that
they can use other strategies they
have learned when responding
to these questions, such as
making connections to personal
experiences or identifying the
main idea. Discuss with students
what the main idea of this story
might be. Then discuss how
students might feel at different
parts of the story if they were
Little Red Riding Hood.

Organize students into pairs. Ask the members of each pair to take turns reading pages or sentences of the story aloud to each other. Have students write down unfamiliar words as they are reading. Encourage them to try to define these words from context. Then have students discuss the meaning of these words with their partners, or help them to define these words.

Big Bad Wolf was still hiding and watching. Big Bad Wolf licked his lips and thought, "Yum, yum. What a big loaf of bread she has. I'm going to follow Little Red Riding Hood. Maybe I'll get a tasty dinner." Little Red Riding Hood walked on.

126

Along the way, she passed the farmer.
The farmer asked, "Where are you
going, Little Red Riding Hood?"
Little Red Riding Hood said, "I'm going
to visit Grandmother."
Then the farmer gave her some ears of
corn to take to Grandmother.

 3 What do you think the Big Bad Wolf will
do next?

127

Possible Responses Question 3

jump out

This is an appropriate prediction based on background knowledge of the traditional tale and a close reading of this selection. Encourage students to write or draw everything that they are thinking about as they read.

eat her

As in the first response, this student is using background knowledge to make a prediction about what might happen next in the story. Ask, "What else could the wolf do besides eat her?"

grab food eat

Students may respond to questions with single related words in a kind of free association. This kind of response not only helps students quickly write down their ideas, but it also helps them summarize what they have read. Encourage this student to clarify his or her response by asking, "What do you think the wolf is going to eat?"

Big Bad Wolf was still hiding and watching.
Big Bad Wolf licked his lips and thought,
"Yum, yum. What big ears of corn she has.
I'm going to follow Little Red Riding Hood.
Maybe I'll get a tasty dinner."
Little Red Riding Hood could not carry
another thing!

 4 What do you think Little Red Riding Hood will do next?

 128

Possible Responses Question 4

drop her food
This is a good prediction that reflects strong reading comprehension. Ask, "What will Little Red Riding Hood do if she drops her food? What can she do instead of dropping her food so she can bring it to Grandmother?"

Cry because I would cry too.
This is a thoughtful response in which the student is empathizing with Little Red Riding Hood and making a prediction based on personal experience. Encourage the student to elaborate on his or her response by asking, "Why would you cry?"

The wolf will get her.
The student offers a good prediction based on background knowledge of the traditional tale, but he or she does not address the question. Say, "That's a very good prediction. What do you think Little Red Riding Hood will do next?"

She stopped and yelled, "Hey, Big Bad Wolf,
I know you're there!
Help me carry all this food to Grandmother.
Then you may stay for dinner."

 5 What do you think the Big Bad Wolf will
do next?

Possible Responses
Question 5

Eat her.

This is a good prediction based on background knowledge and a close reading of the selection. Ask, "What else might happen next?"

run away

This is a clever response in which the student has identified Little Red Riding Hood's ability to stand up for herself and possibly scare the wolf. Encourage the student to elaborate on this response by asking, "Why do you think the wolf will run away?"

eat her dinner

This is a good response in which the student has looked ahead in the reading to predict what the wolf will do next. Ask, "Do you think that the wolf will eat all of Little Red Riding Hood's food, or do you think he will share dinner with Little Red Riding Hood?"

After Reading

It is very important to have students read and discuss the predictions that they wrote in the boxes.

Discussing the Think-Alongs

- Give as many students as possible a chance to tell what they wrote in one of the boxes.
- Have students explain what they were thinking when they wrote.
- Ask students how thinking about what will happen next helps them understand the story.

Reteaching

For those students who have not written or are having difficulty with the activity:

- Ask them to tell what they were thinking about as they read.
- Model your own use of making predictions by telling students what you think might happen next as you read the story aloud.
- Ask questions that motivate students to think about how this story compares with the traditional tale, such as the following:
  - *Have you ever heard the story of Little Red Riding Hood?*
  - *How is this story the same?*
  - *How is this story different?*

Big Bad Wolf did that very thing. From that day on, Big Bad Wolf has been called Big Friendly Wolf.

 130

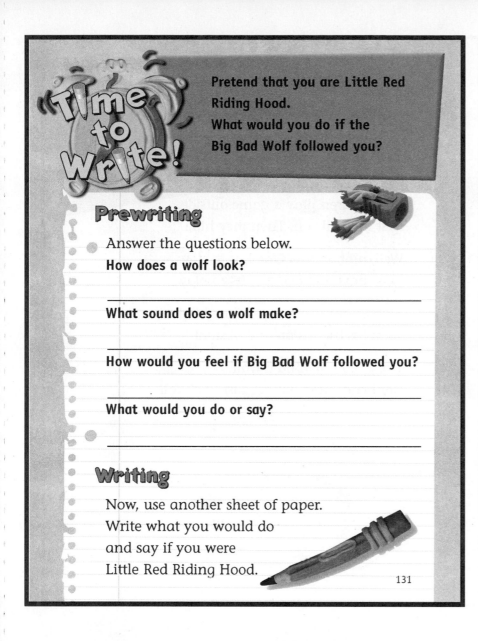

Time to Write!

Pretend that you are Little Red Riding Hood.
What would you do if the Big Bad Wolf followed you?

Prewriting

Answer the questions below.

How does a wolf look?

_____

What sound does a wolf make?

_____

How would you feel if Big Bad Wolf followed you?

_____

What would you do or say?

_____

Writing

Now, use another sheet of paper.
Write what you would do
and say if you were
Little Red Riding Hood.

131

Making Connections

Activity Links

- Ask students to draw pictures that tell the story of another fairy tale. Encourage them to write captions to accompany their illustrations.
- Have students create their own fairy tales. Ask them to write a brief story, and/or draw pictures that illustrate what happens in their fairy tale.
- Have students act out the story of Little Red and the Wolf.
- Have students make puppets of Little Red and the Wolf or another fairy tale, and help them give a puppet show. If possible, invite students from other classes to watch the puppet show.

Reading Links

You may want to include these books in a discussion of unconventional fairy tales:

- *The Frog Prince Continued* by Jon Scieszka (Viking Penguin, 1991).
- *The True Story of the Three Little Pigs* by Jon Scieszka (Viking Penguin, 1989).
- *The Tale of Rabbit and Coyote* by Tony Johnston (The Putnam & Grosset Group, 1994).

Prewriting

Explain to students that the prewriting activity will help them think about how they would feel and what they would say to the Wolf if they were Little Red Riding Hood. Students can work on the prewriting activity individually or in small groups.

Writing

Remind students that they do not have to include everything from the prewriting activity, just the ideas that most help them describe what they would do if they were Little Red Riding Hood.

Sharing

When students have finished the writing activity, ask volunteers to read what they have written and discuss these descriptions with the class.

131

The Tests

The next three selections are similar to standardized-test reading comprehension passages, with questions at the end of each selection. You will be working with students as they progress through the three test sections, which can be administered in different sittings. You can use this test section to provide more practice thinking along by pausing occasionally as you read aloud to ask your students: "What are you thinking about now?" Giving your students this opportunity can help them realize that thinking along can make them better test-takers.

Note that these selections are not designed to test specific reading strategies, but rather are designed to show students how thinking along will help them comprehend and better answer questions about stories.

Introducing the Tests to Students

Tell students that you are going to read some stories aloud and they will answer questions about each story after you have finished reading. Point out that thinking about the story as it is read will make answering questions at the end of the story easier.

Thinking Along on Tests

Read the stories.
Answer the questions.

How do you play this game?
The children play a game outside.
First they all run. Then they hide.

Well, all but one. One has to stay.
They have to have an "It" to play.

Marco counts with eyes closed tight.
Soon his friends are out of sight.

Tracy hides behind a wall.
Her head sticks out because she's tall.

132

Say: *Open your books to page 132.*

Check to be sure all students are on the correct page.

Say: *This story is called "How do you play this game?" Think about that question as we read the story.*

Say: *I will read the story about the game while you follow along. Then I will read it a second time while you follow along again.*

Now listen carefully as I read this story. Follow along in your book.

Read the story aloud. Remember to pause and ask the students to tell what they are thinking—to think along—with the story as you are reading. Next, read the story a second time.

Eric runs off in a dash.
He hides behind the neighbor's trash.

"I'll find you!" Marco gives a shout.
"Oh, no, you won't!" Suzanne cries out.

Marco says, "I think that tree
Just talked. In fact, it yelled at me!"

He tags Suzanne on the other side.
"You're 'It'," he says. "Now I can hide."

Sample: Where was Tracy hiding?

○ behind a tree	○ behind the trash	○ behind a wall

The Selections and Questions

Each of the test sections is followed by four multiple-choice questions and one open-ended question. The question format is typical of many standardized and criterion-referenced tests. The purpose-setting question format at the beginning of each selection is similar to that used on many nationally standardized tests.

Say: *Look at the bottom of the page and find the question that says "Sample."*

Write *Sample* on the chalkboard.

Say: *Put your finger on the sample question and look at the three pictures under the question. Listen carefully as I read you the sample question.*

Sample Question: *"Where was Tracy hiding?"*

- *Was she behind a tree?*
- *Was she behind the trash?*
- *Was she behind a wall?*

Now use your pencil to fill in the circle under the picture that shows where Tracy was hiding in the story.

Demonstrate on the board how the correct answer should be marked. Pause while students mark their answers. Then call on a volunteer to answer the question.

Say: *That's right. In the story Tracy was hiding behind a wall. You will fill in the circle under the picture that shows Tracy behind a wall.*

Check to be sure all students have marked the correct answer. If any have marked under the wrong picture, allow them to erase that circle and fill in the correct circle.

1. Who was "It" when the game began?

○ Suzanne   ○ Tracy   ○ Marco

2. Who is "It" when the story ends?

○ Marco   ○ Suzanne   ○ Eric

3. Why did Marco find Suzanne?

○ She talked.   ○ She ran away.   ○ She is tall.

4. How many players are "It" at one time?

○ one   ○ two   ○ three

134

Say: *Now you will answer the rest of the questions. Find question 1 on this page. Put your finger on question number 1 and listen as I read it.*

Check to see that all students have found question 1.

Say: *Listen carefully as I read you question number 1.*

Question 1: *"Who was 'It' when the game began?"*
• *Was it Suzanne?*
• *Was it Tracy?*
• *Was it Marco?*

Find the picture that shows who was "It." Use your pencil to fill in the circle under the correct picture. Remember, if you change your mind, you can erase your answer and fill in the circle under another picture.

Pause while students mark their answers.

Use these steps to assist students in reading and answering questions 2–4.

5. Where did Eric hide?
Draw a picture. Write about your picture.

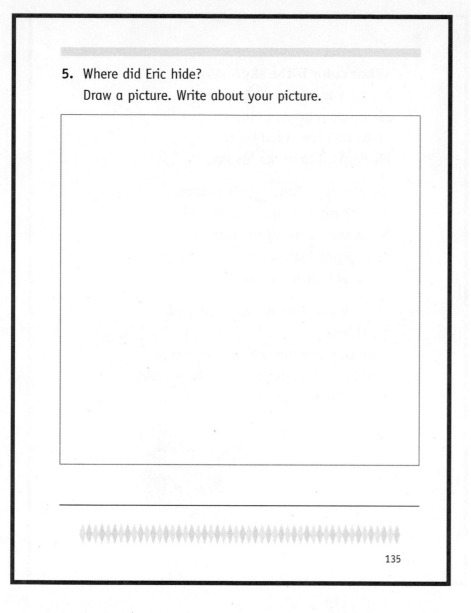

Say: *Now you will draw a picture in the box. The picture will be about a question. Listen carefully and follow along as I read the question.*

Question 5: *"Where did Eric hide?"*
Draw a picture that shows where Eric hid in this story. Try to write some words that tell about your picture on the line at the bottom of the page.

Answers and Analysis

1. Marco; inferential
2. Suzanne; literal
3. She talked. inferential
4. one; inferential
5. Evaluative/critical.

Students' drawings should show Eric hiding behind the trash. Student captions should not be scored but can provide good material for discussion.

Scoring Question 5:

2 = A good drawing will show Eric hiding as described in the story.

0 = A weak drawing will show Eric hiding somewhere other than behind the trash.

Explanation of Comprehension Skills

Literal: The answer is specifically stated in the text.
Inferential: The answer can be inferred from the text, but it is not specifically stated.
Evaluative/Critical: The answer is based on an evaluation of the text.

What color is the sky?

Paulo was making a picture.

He made a green tree.

Then he drew a red barn.

He wanted to make his sky.

Bradley had Paulo's blue crayon.

"That's my crayon," Paulo said.

Nina was drawing her family.

"He's right," she said.

"That is Paulo's crayon."

"I need the crayon," Bradley said.

"It's blue.

I am making the sky on my picture."

"Let Bradley finish his sky," Nina said.

"He won't use all of the blue crayon."

136

Say: *We are going to read another story together. This story is called "What color is the sky?" We will read this story the same way we read the last one. First I will read the story aloud while you follow along, and then I will read it a second time. When we have finished reading, you will answer some questions about the story.*

Look at the top of the page. Now listen carefully as I read this story. Follow along in your book. Put your finger on the place where the story begins.

Read the story aloud. Remember to pause and ask the students to tell what they are thinking—to think along—with the story as you are reading. Next, read the story a second time.

"Look!" Bradley said.
"I have a beautiful blue sky.
But Paulo's sky is yellow!"
"I made a sunny day," Paulo said.
"It is sunny because I get to play with
two good friends."

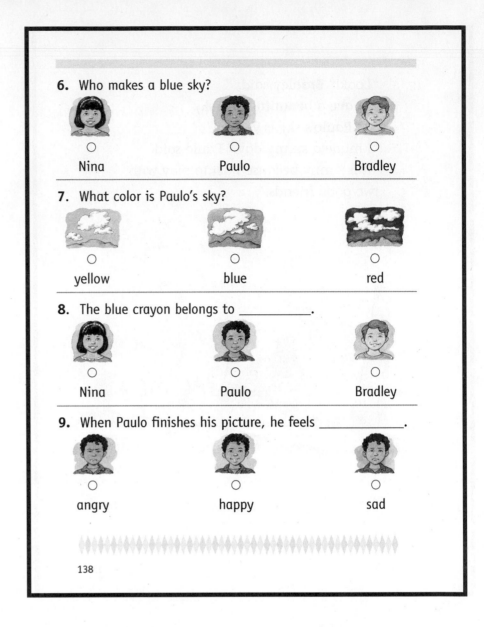

6. Who makes a blue sky?

    ○   ○   ○
  Nina   Paulo   Bradley

7. What color is Paulo's sky?

    ○   ○   ○
  yellow   blue   red

8. The blue crayon belongs to _____.

    ○   ○   ○
  Nina   Paulo   Bradley

9. When Paulo finishes his picture, he feels _____.

    ○   ○   ○
  angry   happy   sad

138

Say: *Now you are going to answer questions about this story. I will read the questions aloud, and you will fill in the circle under the picture that best answers each question.*

Read questions 6–9 one at a time, turning the options under the pictures into questions, such as the following:

Question 6: *"Who makes a blue sky?"*
- *Was it Nina?*
- *Was it Paulo?*
- *Was it Bradley?*
Find the picture and the word that tell who made a blue sky. Use your pencil to fill in the circle under the correct picture. Remember, if you change your mind, you can erase your answer and fill in the circle under another picture.

Walk around the room as you read to verify that students understand how to fill in the appropriate circles. Use these steps to assist students in reading and answering the remaining questions. Pause after reading each question and its answers to give students time to fill in each circle.

10. What was Nina drawing?

Draw a picture. Write about your picture.

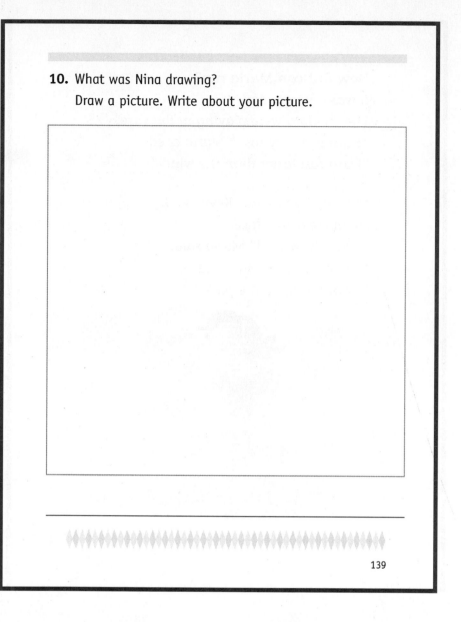

_____

139

Say: _Now you will draw a picture in the box. The picture will be about a question. Listen carefully and follow along as I read the question._

Question 10: _"What was Nina drawing?"_
Draw a picture that shows what Nina was drawing. Try to write some words that tell about your picture on the line at the bottom of the page.

Answers and Analysis

6. Bradley; inferential
7. yellow; literal
8. Paulo; literal
9. happy; evaluative/critical
10. Evaluative/critical.

A correct drawing should show a family. Student captions should not be scored but can provide good material for discussion.

Scoring Question 10:

2 = A good drawing will show a family.

0 = A weak drawing will not show a family.

Explanation of Comprehension Skills

Literal: The answer is specifically stated in the text.

Inferential: The answer can be inferred from the text, but it is not specifically stated.

Evaluative/Critical: The answer is based on an evaluation of the text.

How fast can Maria run?
It was a windy day.
The children were playing in the yard.
"I can run very fast!" Maria cried.
"I can run faster than the wind!"

"Oh, sure you can," Kevin said.
He made a silly face.
"I can show you!" Maria said.
"Oh, come on!" Matt said.
"I want to go to the park."

140

Say: *We are going to read one more story together. This story is called "How fast can Maria run?" We will read this story the same way we read the others. First I will read the story aloud while you follow along, and then I will read it a second time. When we have finished reading, you will answer some questions about the story.*

Look at the top of the page. Now listen carefully as I read this story about Maria. Follow along in your book. Put your finger on the place where the story begins.

Read the story about Maria aloud. Remember to pause and ask the students to tell what they are thinking—to think along—with the story as you are reading. Next, read the story a second time.

"Just watch me!" Maria cried.
She ran into the house.
Maria looked out a window.
"Is it still windy out there?" she asked.
"Yes," Matt said.
"Well, there's no wind in here," she said.
"She beat the wind inside," Kevin said.

Maria stuck her head out the window.
The wind blew her hair all around.
"Oh, boy!" Matt said.
"The wind does not like losing."

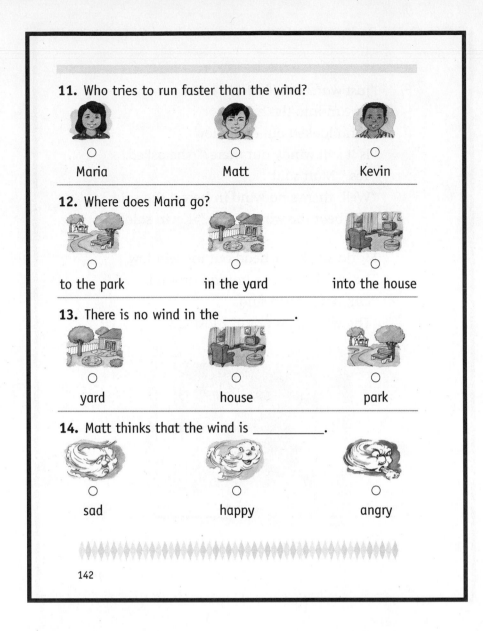

11. Who tries to run faster than the wind?

○ Maria   ○ Matt   ○ Kevin

12. Where does Maria go?

○ to the park   ○ in the yard   ○ into the house

13. There is no wind in the _____.

○ yard   ○ house   ○ park

14. Matt thinks that the wind is _____.

○ sad   ○ happy   ○ angry

142

Say: *Now you are going to answer questions about this story. I will read the questions aloud, and you will fill in the circles under the picture that best answers each question.*

Read questions 11–14 one at a time, turning the options under the pictures into questions, such as the following:

Question 11: *"Who tries to run faster than the wind?"*
- *Is it Maria?*
- *Is it Matt?*
- *Is it Kevin?*
Find the picture and the word that tell who the runner is. Use your pencil to fill in the circle under the correct picture. Remember, if you change your mind you can erase your answer and fill in the circle under another picture.

Walk around the room as you read to verify that students understand how to fill in the appropriate circles. Use these steps to assist students in reading and answering the remaining questions. Pause after reading each question and its answers to give students time to fill in each circle.

15. Where did Matt want to go?
Draw a picture. Write about your picture.

143

Discussion

After students have completed all three tests and you have graded them, give them back to students and review the questions and the correct answers. Read each story aloud once and then read each question, letting volunteers give the correct answers. Have students share their drawings with the class.

Scoring

Refer to the discussion of test taking on page T11 of the teacher's edition for information on scoring and interpreting student scores.

Say: *Now you will draw a picture in the box. The picture will be about a question. Listen carefully and follow along as I read the question.*

Question 15: *"Where did Matt want to go?"*
Draw a picture that shows where Matt wanted to go. Try to write some words that tell about your picture on the line at the bottom of the page.

Answers and Analysis

11. Maria; literal
12. into the house; literal
13. house; inferential
14. angry; evaluative/critical
15. Evaluative/critical.
A correct drawing should show a park. Student captions should not be scored but can provide good material for discussion.

Scoring Question 15:

2 = A good drawing will show a park.
0 = A weak drawing will show something else besides a park.

Explanation of Comprehension Skills

Literal: The answer is specifically stated in the text.
Inferential: The answer can be inferred from the text, but it is not specifically stated.
Evaluative/Critical: The answer is based on an evaluation of the text.

Acknowledgments

Grateful acknowledgment is made to the following authors and publishers for the use of copyrighted materials. Every effort has been made to obtain permission to use previously published material. Any errors or omissions are unintentional.

All Kinds of Wheels by Stephanie Handwerker. Copyright © 1997 by Steck-Vaughn Company.

Bears, Bears, and More Bears by Jackie Morris. Copyright © 1995. Reprinted by arrangement with Barron's Educational Series, Inc., Hauppage, New York.

A Fishy Story by Richard Leslie. Copyright © 1997 by Steck-Vaughn Company.

Going to the Pool by Ena Keo. Copyright © 1997 by Steck-Vaughn Company.

Little Red and the Wolf by Gare Thompson. Copyright © 1997 by Steck-Vaughn Company.

My Boat by Kay Davies and Wendy Oldfield (Gareth Stevens, Inc.). By permission of Gareth Stevens, Inc. Copyright © A&C Black (Publishers) Ltd.

My New Boy by Joan Phillips. Text copyright © 1986 by Joan Phillips. Illustrations copyright © 1986 by Lynn Munsinger. Reprinted by arrangement with Random House, Inc.

My Sister Is My Friend by Hannah Markley. From SIGNATURES, EMERGENT READERS: MY SISTER IS MY FRIEND, copyright © 1995 by Harcourt Brace & Company. Reprinted by permission of the publisher.

Pet Day by Lois Bick. From SIGNATURES, INSTANT READERS: PET DAY, Grade 1, copyright © 1996 by Harcourt Brace & Company. Reprinted by permission of the publisher.

Sam's Seasons by Christine Price. Copyright © 1997 by Steck-Vaughn Company.

So Can I by Margery Facklam. Text copyright © 1988 by Margery Facklam. Illustration copyright © 1988 by Jeni Bassett. Reprinted by permission of Harcourt Brace & Company.

From *Soccer Game!* by Grace Maccarone, illustrated by Meredith Johnson. A Hello Reader! Book published by Cartwheel Books, a division of Scholastic Inc. Text copyright © 1994 by Grace Maccarone, illustrations copyright © 1994 by Meredith Johnson. Reprinted by permission of Scholastic Inc. HELLO READER! and CARTWHEEL BOOKS are registered trademarks of Scholastic Inc.

"The Surprise Party" by Mary Cockett. From *Away Went the Hat and Other Stories* by Mary Cockett. Copyright © 1989 by Thomas Nelson & Sons, Ltd. Reprinted by permission of the author.

There Is a Town by Gail Herman. Text copyright © 1996 by Gail Herman. Illustrations copyright © 1996 by Katy Bratun. Reprinted by arrangement with Random House, Inc.

Whistle Like a Bird by Sarah Vazquez. Copyright © 1997 by Steck-Vaughn Company.

Illustration Credits

Terry Kovalcik, p. T16; Rick Garcia, pp. T17–T20; Judith DuFour Love, pp. T21–T24; Francisco Mora, pp. T25–T28; Ken Bowser, pp. 4, 5, 34, 35, 70, 96; Jeni Bassett, cover, pp. 6–14; Katy Bratun, pp. 16–22; Jackie Morris, pp. 24–32; Larry Johnson, cover, pp. 36–40; Winifred Barnum-Newman, cover, pp. 50–56; Steve Henry, pp. 58–60, 62–64, 66–68; Meredith Johnson, pp. 72–78; Shirley Bellwood, pp. 81–85; Wallace Keller, cover, pp. 88–94; Lynn Munsinger, pp. 110–120; Nan Brooks, cover, pp. 122–130; Mike Krone, pp. 132–134, 136–138, 140–142.

Photography Credits

Cover (front) Sam Dudgeon; cover (back) © Steven Raymer; p. T4 © Jeff Dunn/Stock Boston; p. T5 © Steven Raymer; p. T8a Cindi Ellis; p. T8b Ian Shaw/Tony Stone Images; pp. T12–T15, 5, 35 Rick Williams; p. 42 © Joe Szkodzinski/Image Bank; p. 43 © John Rich; p. 44 © John Elk/Stock Boston; p. 45 © Susan Van Etten; p. 46 © Park Street; p. 47 © David Hamilton/Image Bank; p. 48a © Joe Szkodzinski/Image Bank; p. 48b © John Rich; p. 48c © John Elk/Stock Boston; p. 48d © Susan Van Etten; p. 48e © Park Street; p. 48f © David Hamilton/Image Bank; p. 71 Rick Williams; p. 97 Rick Williams; pp. 98, 99, 100, 101, 102, 103, 104, 105, 106, 107, 108 © 1990 Fiona Pragoff.